HOW, WHY AND WHERE

DO MEN AND WOMEN CHEAT ON EACH OTHER

HOW, WHY AND WHERE

DO MEN AND WOMEN CHEAT ON EACH OTHER

R.E. GEFFNER MD

Imar Publishing

ISBN (Paperback): 979-8-9991712-9-0
ISBN (eBook): 979-8-9952823-0-3

Book Design by the Aaxel Author Group

Cover artwork by Vincent-Louis Apruzzese

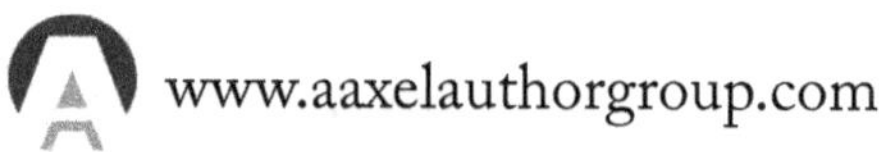 www.aaxelauthorgroup.com

Dedication

To those who have betrayed and to those who have been betrayed.

To the husbands and wives who reached outside their relationship,
not because they were evil, selfish, or reckless,
but because they were starving for attention, affection, safety,
or even the simple feeling of being seen.

To the partners who felt blindsided by infidelity
and wondered how they missed the warning signs,
who blamed themselves,
who blamed the other,
and who eventually realized that heartbreak is rarely born from
one moment,
but from many small unmet needs over time.

To the people who hurt someone they loved
because they themselves were hurting,
lonely, exhausted, unappreciated,
or afraid of disappearing in their own home.

To those who didn't cheat physically,

but drifted emotionally,
slowly replacing connection with resentment,
and curiosity with silence.

To the couples who learned the hard truth:
No one breaks a healthy relationship.
They only escape one that has been dying quietly.

There are no heroes or villains here.
There are only human beings
with needs, insecurities, desires, and limits.

This book is for both of you,
for the one who stepped outside the relationship
and the one who did not see the distance growing.

For the partners who are willing to look at each other honestly
instead of pretending one person carries all the blame.

May you both find compassion, not punishment.
May you learn why the bond cracked,
instead of arguing about who hit it first.
And may this knowledge help you heal,
whether that healing happens together or apart.

Table of Contents

Dedication v

Mission Statement xi

Preface xvi

Introduction xix

Part I   How Men Cheat on Women **1**

Emotional Ways

Chapter 1   Confidante at Work: When Safety Becomes Seduction 3

Chapter 2   Emotional Texting/Direct Messaging: The Affair in Your Hand 6

Chapter 3   Trauma Bonding: When Feeling Unseen Leads Him Elsewhere 11

Chapter 4   Reconnecting With an Ex: Nostalgia Disguised as "Just Checking In" 13

Chapter 5   Online Emotional Intimacy: When Screens Become Safer Than Real Life 15

Chapter 6   Seeking Admiration: The Ego's Affair 17

Chapter 7   Emotional Affairs Through Hobbies: When Shared Interests Become Shared Hearts 19

Chapter 8   Using a Female Friend as a Therapist: When Venting Becomes Betrayal 21

Chapter 9   Love-Bombing Another Woman: Compliments, Gifts, Emotional Idealization, and the Fantasy Future   24

Chapter 10   Secret "Platonic" Friendships   27

Sexual Ways

Chapter 11   Transactional Sex: Escorts, Massage Parlors, and the Illusion of No Emotional Consequences   30

Chapter 12   One-Night Stands: Bars, Trips, Bachelor Weekends, and Conferences   33

Chapter 13   Sugar Arrangements: Financial Support in Exchange for Intimacy   36

Chapter 14   Porn Addiction Replacing Intimacy: Compulsive Use, Cam Models, and Live Chat   39

Chapter 15   Sexual Texting or Sexting: Photos, Videos, and Digital Sexuality   42

Chapter 16   Workplace Sex: When Professional Proximity Turns Into Physical Betrayal   45

Chapter 17   Sex Tourism: "Out of Town" as an Excuse for No Consequences   48

Chapter 18   Micro-Cheating in Person: Grabbing, Touching, and Grinding at Clubs   51

Chapter 19   Using Dating Apps: "Just Browsing," Swiping, Talking, and Hooking Up   54

Part II How Women Cheat on Men   57

Emotional Ways

Chapter 20   Emotional Replacement: Women Forming a Deep
              Connection With a Man Who Listens and
              Validates Her   58

Chapter 21   Fantasy Relationship: Imagining a Life With
              Someone Else, Romantic Daydreaming   61

Chapter 22   Affair of the Heart With a Coworker: Sharing
              Details She Denies Her Husband   65

Chapter 23   Reconnecting With an Old Flame: Nostalgia,
              Messages, "I Wonder What Could've Been."   70

Chapter 24   Validation From Compliments: Living on
              Attention From Male Friends or Strangers   74

Chapter 25   Venting to Another Man About Her Marriage:
              Emotional Betrayal Disguised as Friendship   78

Chapter 26   The "Work Husband" or Gym Partner: Comfort,
              Partnership, Inside Jokes, and the Disappearance
              of Boundaries   82

Chapter 27   Posting Seductive Photos: Not for Her Husband,
              but for Other Men   87

Chapter 28   Online Emotional Bonds: DMs, Comments, and
              Long Digital Relationships   92

Chapter 29   Secret Friendships: Hiding Them Because She
              Knows Her Husband Wouldn't Approve   97

Sexual Ways

Chapter 30   Physical Affair: Sexual Encounters With Someone Else   101

Chapter 31   Revenge Sex: Cheating Because She Felt Betrayed, Neglected, or Hurt   106

Chapter 32   Sexual Texting and Photos: Sending Nudes, Sexting, and Explicit Messages   110

Chapter 33   Affairs With "Safe" Male Friends: The Guy She Insists Is "Just a Friend"   115

Chapter 34   Sex During Business Trips: Conferences, Retreats, and Vacations With Friends   117

Chapter 35   Hookups With Exes: Comfortable, Familiar With Low Emotional Risk   120

Chapter 36   Sex for Validation: Using Intimacy to Feel Wanted, Powerful, and Admired   123

Chapter 37   Digital Escorts/Cam Interactions: Paying or Receiving Sexual Attention Online   126

Chapter 38   Club Hookups: Kissing, Touching, Grinding, and Sexual Contact in Nightlife Settings   129

Chapter 39   Using Dating Apps: "Just Talking," Curiosity, Flirting, Then Progressing to Sex   132

Epilogue   The Roads Back to Ourselves   135

About the Author   141

Mission Statement

This book is for anyone who still believes that love is worth saving before it slips away.

Nobody who opens these pages should ever again feel like they've missed the boat. Armed with what you learn here, you can take the first step toward reclaiming what matters.

That first step begins with AIR:

Awareness is the ability to honestly see what is happening, especially the parts we once ignored, misunderstood, or minimized. When we become aware, we stop reacting blindly and begin to understand the truth of a situation.

Intention is what follows awareness. It is the desire and commitment to take action based on what you now see. Intention is not a vague wish; it is a conscious decision to respond differently, to move toward healing instead of repeating old patterns.

Repair is the practice of fixing what has been hurt, broken, or neglected. Repair does not mean perfection; it means restoring connection, rebuilding trust, and improving how we treat ourselves and others.

Together, **Awareness + Intention + Repair = AIR.**

Just as we cannot live without the air we breathe, healthy relationships cannot breathe without this process. When you use AIR as your guide, your relationships become clearer, calmer, and more nourishing—allowing you to rest easier, communicate better, and sleep with peace instead of anxiety.

This book will equip you with the awareness to recognize what is truly happening in your relationships, the motivation to act with intention, and the tools and skills to create meaningful change. Although no system can promise perfection, following this guide will become the closest thing to a roadmap, one that can profoundly improve the relationship between you and the person you love.

This book will help you develop a deep awareness of your relational patterns. Every human bond—romantic, familial, professional, or social—is shaped by unseen dynamics of perception, emotion, reaction, and expectation. These forces constantly move between people, influencing how we speak, how we listen, how we connect, and how we hurt. Most of us navigate these interactions on autopilot, responding from habit rather than understanding. This book teaches you to slow down, see clearly, and finally understand the deeper emotional currents at play.

Awareness is the first stage of transformation.

When you begin to recognize the patterns in human behavior—yours and others'—you gain a clearer understanding of the direction your relationship needs to grow. Awareness gives you a map: It shows you where you stand, what needs attention, and what choices will move you forward.

My mission in this book is to provide the tools, skills, and practical guidance necessary to strengthen your connections, deepen communication, and transform the way you relate to others. **By applying these principles, you will move beyond merely understanding your relationships; you will develop the ability to shape them intentionally into healthier, stronger, and more fulfilling bonds.**

Unless we live in complete isolation, we are constantly participating in relationships. Every interaction, be it through word, gesture, silence, misunderstanding, or a moment of affection, creates an emotional and psychological response. Our minds interpret these moments, assign them meaning, and react to them, often without our conscious awareness. Over time, these interpretations accumulate and form the blueprint for how we love, argue, forgive, protect ourselves, draw close, or pull away. They become the invisible architecture of our relational lives. This work aims to expand our understanding of how interactions function. It invites readers to see relationships not as fixed or mysterious but as dynamic systems that can be understood, improved, and transformed.

Awareness is only the beginning. Once we understand the deeper mechanics of our interactions, we can intentionally shape them. We can learn new patterns, replace old ones, communicate more honestly, love more deeply, and build relationships that thrive rather than fracture.

This book and the entire *Foundation of Healthy Relationships* series are dedicated to helping people begin that journey with clarity, compassion, and practical guidance.

As a physician, I have gained not only extensive theoretical knowledge but also deep, practical wisdom through real-world encounters with people and their struggles. In my years of medical practice, I have witnessed how stress, fear, communication breakdowns, and family conflict manifest in the body. I have seen firsthand the emotional pressures that relationships place on a person's health, how unresolved tension becomes insomnia, how loneliness becomes fatigue, how resentment becomes pain, and how unspoken feelings eventually become symptoms.

I've watched couples argue at their bedside, families fall apart, partners struggle to support each other, and individuals suffer silently because they don't know how to express what they feel. I've listened to patients confide things they could never tell their spouse, partner, or even closest friends.

I'm not speaking about relationships from a distance. I've witnessed up close how emotional disconnection affects health, how unresolved conflict shows up physically, and how loneliness in a relationship can be as painful as any medical condition.

Through these experiences, I have developed an understanding of human behavior and the emotional patterns people fall into. These experiences have also given me the tools to recognize these sufferings quickly and guide people toward healthier communication, stronger emotional bonds, and more supportive partnerships.

For these reasons, I am uniquely qualified to address the struggles explored in this book and throughout the *Foundation of Healthy Relationships* series, not only from a theoretical or academic perspective but also through years of sitting with real people in real pain. I have witnessed their fear, confusion, and emotional exhaustion and have helped them find their way back to clarity, connection, and healing. My insights come from lived clinical experience, not abstract concepts. Each principle in these pages has been shaped by the stories, challenges, and recoveries of those who trusted me with their lives and hearts.

Having evolved through this process, I have been inspired to expand my focus, leading to the creation of the *Foundation of Healthy Relationships* series, which will be accompanied by workshops, clinical input from psychologists, and accessible tools for individuals, couples, and families. My goal is to use this work to strengthen relationships nationwide, reduce the social and personal costs of family breakdowns, and empower communities to thrive.

The *Foundation of Healthy Relationships* series is a multi-volume collection created to heal, strengthen, and elevate relationships at every stage of life. These books were written with a single mission: to give individuals the tools, insights, and skills necessary to build significant relationships.

This series is built on the core belief that relationships don't fall apart because people don't care. They fall apart because most people have never been taught how to: express emotions clearly; repair after conflict; build trust intentionally; nurture intimacy and affection; communicate needs without fear; understand hormonal, psychological, and biological differences; prevent resentment before it grows; and turn daily interactions into daily investments.

The *Foundation of Healthy Relationships* series is a transformational collection for couples, families, and individuals seeking lasting love, emotional mastery, and relationship wisdom.

Preface

Who cheats more on each other, men or women? The numbers have changed. Why?

1. Technology

Direct Messaging.

Instagram, Snapchat, TikTok, and dating apps.

Women no longer have to "wait" to be approached. Attention is *delivered to their phone*.

A woman can wake up to 20 compliments a day from strangers. This is fuel for emotional connection:

> "You look gorgeous."
> "I wish my girlfriend dressed like that."
> "Your husband is so lucky."

2. Workplace environments

Women now work in offices, teams, sales, travel, and corporate retreats.

Exactly where men historically cheated.

3. Emotional deprivation

Men often complain about sex disappearing.

Women complain about the connection disappearing.

When a woman meets someone who listens, asks about her life, makes her feel seen, remembers her details, and compliments her efforts. She emotionally steps out of the marriage before she physically does.

Men cheat more for ego.

"I still got it."

"She wanted me."

"She was available."

Women cheat more for connection.

"He listened."

"He understood."

"He saw me."

So who cheats more often today?

If we measure *sexual infidelity*:
Men still slightly lead.
If we measure *emotional infidelity*:
Women lead by a wide margin.

And emotional cheating is not "less harmful." Often, it is worse. A woman can sleep with someone once and forget them. But if she bonds emotionally, she is gone for good.

A brutal observation therapists repeat: A man cheats to *escape* his relationship. A woman cheats because she emotionally *left* the relationship long ago.

Neither is morally superior. Both are rooted in unmet needs, poor communication, and emotional dysregulation. The real question is not about who cheats more. It is about how and why.

Love rarely dies from a single betrayal. It decays one boundary at a time: when attention leaves the relationship, when intimacy becomes routine, when conversations turn into arguments, and when partners begin seeking validation anywhere except from each other.

In every culture and every era, infidelity has existed. Not because we are weak, but because we are human. Humans ache to feel seen, admired, respected, and desired. When those needs go unmet, many drift into emotional affairs, secret connections, private fantasies, and eventually, sexual betrayal. The tragedy is that most cheating does not begin with lust. It begins with loneliness.

A marriage is not broken by the moment someone lies in another bed, but by the months or years of emotional neglect that precede it. Cheating is not an accident; it is a symptom. A symptom of silence, resentment, trauma, fear, unmet needs, and the absence of repair.

This book is not written to shame or condemn you. It is written to help you understand the deeper emotional mechanics behind infidelity—why men cheat, why women cheat, how emotional affairs begin, and why sexual affairs are often the final expression of a long-ignored wound.

> If you are here, your pain is real.
> Maybe you are the betrayed.
> Maybe you are the betrayer.
> Maybe you are both.

Whatever your story, I want you to know something very simple: **you are not alone.** And your relationship is not beyond help. The moment you understand the emotional anatomy of cheating, you also gain the tools to heal, rebuild, or finally walk away with dignity.

This book will not promise perfection; it will deliver clarity. It will show you how infidelity takes root, how it grows in secrecy, and how to reclaim power through awareness, intention, and repair.

Not all relationships can be saved. But many could have been saved if one person had learned to speak before the other learned to cheat.

Introduction

Cheating is never just about sex. It is about connection.

When a man cheats, it often begins with admiration. Someone laughs at his jokes, listens to his dreams, and makes him feel capable again. He begins texting, sharing his frustrations, opening doors he has long closed. Weeks pass, and he tells himself it is harmless, "we're just talking." He feels alive, powerful, desired. And then one day, a line is crossed.

When a woman cheats, it often begins with emotional starvation. She starts confiding in a coworker who actually listens. He remembers her birthdays, compliments her hair, and validates her efforts. The conversations feel intimate, comforting, and safe. She tells herself, "I deserve to feel appreciated." And eventually, she steps into the arms of the person who heard her heart before her husband did.

Men frequently seek cheating through ego. Women frequently seek cheating through connection. Different roads, same destination: betrayal.

Infidelity is not gendered. It does not belong to men or women; it belongs to pain.

This book explores the two primary pathways of cheating:

1. Emotional Infidelity

The overlooked, underestimated beginning:

Late-night messages
Heart-to-heart conversations
Fantasy bonds
Emotional replacement
Online intimacy
"Just friends" with hidden intentions

Emotional infidelity always starts with a redirect of energy. When your private thoughts, vulnerabilities, and hopes are shared with someone outside the relationship, you have already replaced your partner.

2. Sexual Infidelity

The outcome:

Physical affairs
One-night encounters
Workplace hookups
Revenge sex
Porn and cam interactions that become an obsession
Dating apps that are designed to "just talk."

Sex is the final step of a process that began long before bare skin ever touched.

We will examine:

- Why men cheat and the emotional gaps they try to fill.
- Why women cheat and the emotional starvation that leads them there.
- How trauma, childhood wounds, and validation hunger turn desire into addiction.
- How modern technology accelerates infidelity at the pace of a swipe.

- How to recognize the signs long before betrayal is visible.
- How to save a relationship, if it should be saved.
- How to rebuild trust or walk away with dignity and self-respect.

Most importantly, this book will guide you away from blame and toward understanding—because blame fuels hate and understanding fuels healing.

You will learn the anatomy of cheating:

The moment emotional energy leaves the marriage.

The moment secrecy replaces honesty.

The moment intention becomes action.

And the moment the betrayer becomes a stranger.

This is not a book about villains and victims. It is a book about humans, imperfect, wounded, yearning for connection.

If you have been betrayed, you will find validation.

If you have betrayed, you will find accountability.

If you want to prevent infidelity, you will find tools.

Whether you stay, repair, or reclaim your life alone, may this book be your truth, your awakening, and perhaps your second chance.

Part I

How Men Cheat on Women

Emotional Ways

Chapter 1   Confidante at Work: When Safety Becomes Seduction   3

Chapter 2   Emotional Texting/Direct Messaging: The Affair in Your Hand   6

Chapter 3   Trauma Bonding: When Feeling Unseen Leads Him Elsewhere   11

Chapter 4   Reconnecting With an Ex: Nostalgia Disguised as "Just Checking In"   13

Chapter 5   Online Emotional Intimacy: When Screens Become Safer Than Real Life   15

Chapter 6   Seeking Admiration: The Ego's Affair   17

Chapter 7   Emotional Affairs Through Hobbies: When Shared Interests Become Shared Hearts   19

Chapter 8   Using a Female Friend as a Therapist: When Venting
            Becomes Betrayal   21

Chapter 9   Love-Bombing Another Woman: Compliments, Gifts,
            Emotional Idealization, and the Fantasy Future   24

Chapter 10   Secret "Platonic" Friendships   27

Sexual Ways

Chapter 11   Transactional Sex: Escorts, Massage Parlors, and
            the Illusion of No Emotional Consequences   30

Chapter 12   One-Night Stands: Bars, Trips, Bachelor
            Weekends, and Conferences   33

Chapter 13   Sugar Arrangements: Financial Support in
            Exchange for Intimacy   36

Chapter 14   Porn Addiction Replacing Intimacy: Compulsive
            Use, Cam Models, and Live Chat   39

Chapter 15   Sexual Texting or Sexting: Photos, Videos, and
            Digital Sexuality   42

Chapter 16   Workplace Sex: When Professional Proximity
Turns Into Physical Betrayal   45

Chapter 17   Sex Tourism: "Out of Town" as an Excuse for No
            Consequences   48

Chapter 18   Micro-Cheating in Person: Grabbing, Touching,
            and Grinding at Clubs   51

Chapter 19   Using Dating Apps: "Just Browsing," Swiping,
            Talking, and Hooking Up   54

Chapter 1

Confidante at Work: When Safety Becomes Seduction

Infidelity does not always begin in the bedroom. Often, it begins in the fluorescent glow of an office, during lunch breaks, in conference rooms, or during quiet moments after deadlines. It is born in conversations where vulnerability is shared not with a spouse, but with someone who feels just a little easier to talk to. He tells himself it's harmless. Just a coworker. Just a friend.But the truth is far more silent and far more dangerous: the emotional intimacy that should have been nurtured at home is now being cultivated somewhere else.

At first, it is subtle:

> Complaints about stressful meetings.
> A shared laugh over the absurdity of work politics.
> A sympathetic nod when he talks about how exhausted he is.

Then, something shifts.

Instead of telling his wife about the difficult argument he

had at work, he tells her.

Instead of sharing his career dreams or frustrations with his partner, he confides in her.

Instead of saying good morning to his wife, he looks forward to seeing "her smile" at the office.

The coworker becomes the person whom *he trusts, updates, and emotionally depends on.*

He rationalizes it:

"She just understands me."

"We work in the same industry."

"It's easier to talk to someone who isn't judging."

But intimacy is not defined by sex—it is defined by access.

The moment he gives this woman access to his inner world, she is no longer a colleague. She is now the emotional partner. The betrayal has already begun.

Not because of lust.

Not because of physical contact.

But because the foundation of partnership—emotional exclusivity—has been outsourced to someone who is not his spouse.

Why this happens

Many men do not cheat because they want to. They cheat because they feel:

- Unseen
- Unappreciated
- Misunderstood
- Dismissed or criticized at home

Trapped in responsibility without admiration. Work becomes a stage where he performs well, competently, capably, and charmingly. And she becomes his audience. Every nod, every compliment, every "I get it" becomes fuel. He begins to chase the way he feels around her, not the woman herself.

How a confidante turns into an affair

1. Emotional vulnerability
2. Secrets
3. Personal frustrations
4. Compliments
5. Private jokes
6. Birthday lunches
7. One-on-one meetings
8. After-work drinks

What started as comfort becomes habit.
What started as habit becomes dependence.
What started as dependence becomes desire.

By the time he realizes it, he has rewritten his emotional allegiance:

He no longer comes home to talk.
He comes home to rest.
He talks to her to live.

And in that moment, the affair has already happened, whether there has been physical contact or not. Because cheating is not defined by sex. It is defined by the *redirection of emotional intimacy* to someone outside the relationship.

Chapter 2

Emotional Texting/ Direct Messaging: The Affair in Your Hand

Cheating does not begin with a hotel room. It begins with a notification.

A small vibration in the pocket.
A message that reads:
"You're so funny, lol."
"I can't sleep."
"Tell me more."

Late-night conversations become the new intimacy. The person on the other end of the screen becomes a mirror, a comfort, a source of validation. And, most dangerously, they become the place you go to feel alive.

It starts as harmless:

An Instagram reaction to a story
A casual work-related text
A meme
An inside joke.

Then the tone shifts.

"Long day?"
"Wish I could talk to someone like you about this."
"You're different."
"You get me."

And in that moment, the digital gate opens.

How emotional affairs hide in technology

Unlike physical cheating, emotional cheating via DMs is invisible, quiet, and clean.

No perfume.
No lipstick.
No hotel receipts.
Only screenshots, and even those can be deleted.

Phones become secret bedrooms.

In bed next to their partner, they are miles away, typing, laughing, sending voice notes. They say, "We're just talking." But conversations become flirtation, flirtation becomes anticipation, anticipation becomes obsession. This is not harmless. It is *pre-affair intimacy*. Because when your phone lights up and your heart skips a beat for someone who is not your spouse, the betrayal has already started.

Why emotional texting is so powerful

Unlike face-to-face affairs, digital intimacy allows a person to curate the best version of themselves.

No morning breath.
No messy arguments.
No bills.
No responsibilities.

Only praise, attention, laughter, and fantasy. It is the edited version of love—highlight reels of longing without the weight of real life.

Texting offers something even more intoxicating than sex: a continuous supply of validation.

Every ding is a dopamine hit:

"She thought of me."
"He wants to talk again."
"They're waiting for my reply."

Humans do not become addicted to people. They become addicted to *how those people make them feel.*

The language of emotional cheating

Affairs rarely begin with "I want you." They begin with:

"I can't talk to my wife the way I talk to you."
"I wish my husband listened the way you do."
"You understand me better than anyone."
"Don't tell anyone, but…"

These are emotional vows disguised as vulnerability.
They feel:

Intimate
Exclusive
Rebellious
Forbidden
Special

And the more secrets are shared, the more the secrecy itself becomes erotic. You don't need a bed to cheat. You just need someone who answers every time you feel empty.

When texting crosses the line

Not every casual chat is betrayal. But there is a moment when the line is crossed, and it is unmistakable: *the texting becomes something you hide.*

When messages are cleared.

When names are changed in the contacts.

When the phone is flipped screen-down on the table.

When the partner walks into the room and silence replaces laughter.

The deception is not in the content; it is in the secrecy.

Cheating begins the moment you start editing your truth.

The emotional escalation

1. Conversation
2. Attention
3. Attachment
4. Validation
5. Dependence
6. Fantasy
7. Physical invitation

By the time their fingers meet in person, the hearts have already crossed the line. Sex merely confirms what the soul already did.

Why people don't see this as cheating

Because society measures infidelity by bodies—not by hearts. A person will swear:

"We never touched."
"We're just friends."
"You're overreacting."
"You're insecure.

But the betrayed partner knows the truth: they didn't lose them to a body, they lost them to a screen. Emotional texting is the slow erosion of loyalty. It is the secret romance without the consequences. It is the affair you can fight with your thumbs. And it can destroy a relationship just as powerfully as sex ever could.

Chapter 3

Trauma Bonding: When Feeling Unseen Leads Him Elsewhere

When "she understands me" feels like salvation

Trauma bonding is not the dramatic scene of two people surviving a car crash or a life-threatening event together. In relationships, it is far quieter. It occurs when a man feels chronically misunderstood, dismissed, or invisible at home, and finds emotional refuge in a woman who listens without judgment. She becomes the place he goes not just to talk—but to breathe. She hears him describe the stress he carries, the pressure he feels, the resentment he never dares speak at home. She validates his worries, praises his efforts, and tells him he deserves better. Soon, the connection becomes addictive, not because she is extraordinary, but because she is attentive in the exact spaces where he feels neglected. He convinces himself, "She sees me. She gets me. She understands me." And with every vulnerable confession, every emotional disclosure, he unconsciously deepens the bond.

Trauma bonding thrives on unmet emotional needs. When a

partner at home responds with criticism, dismissal, or exhaustion, he internalizes failure: "I'm not enough." But when another woman responds with empathy—"You're doing so much," "I don't know how you handle it all," "You're incredible for carrying so much"—he feels seen. His nervous system relaxes. Validation becomes medicine. And like any medicine, it becomes something he craves. What started as a safe space becomes a dependency. He stops talking to his wife about disappointments, stress, anxieties, or childhood wounds. He shares them with the other woman instead. She becomes the emotional healer; the wife, the emotional obstacle.

The danger of trauma bonding is that it masquerades as authenticity. He tells himself it's not cheating—he's simply confiding, opening up, "finally being himself." But emotional intimacy is the currency of relationships, and the moment it is invested elsewhere, betrayal has already begun. This type of affair is more powerful than sexual attraction because it is spiritual: two people bonding over pain, vulnerability, and a shared sense of "us against the world." He does not fall in love with her body; he falls in love with the version of himself he becomes when he is with her. And by the time he realizes the depth of the connection, it is no longer about escape—it is about survival.

Chapter 4

Reconnecting With an Ex: Nostalgia Disguised as "Just Checking In"

Infidelity does not always come from strangers. Sometimes it comes from someone who once knew your heartbeat.

Reconnecting with an ex is a unique emotional poison because it bypasses the awkwardness of a new attraction. There is no need to impress, no small talk, no introduction of childhood stories or preferences. The history already exists. The roles were already defined. The emotional blueprint is there, waiting to be reactivated. All it takes is a birthday message, a random "Hey stranger," or a quiet, seemingly harmless, "I was just thinking about you."

Unlike a new fling, nostalgia arrives wearing the mask of innocence.

"I just want closure."

"We're just catching up."

"It's not a big deal."

But behind those messages is a dangerous truth:
The past never returns empty-handed.

The ex becomes a symbol of who he used to be—before bills, responsibilities, marriage, children, and adult exhaustion. She reminds him of youth, freedom, possibility, the earlier version of himself he misses more than he misses her. Their conversations are drenched in selective memory: the best nights, the laughter, the affection, the sex, the dreams they once shared. The conflicts, the breakups, the heartbreak—those get edited out. Nostalgia is not truth; it is memory with all the pain removed.

What begins as "just checking in" quickly turns emotional. She asks how he's doing.She remembers the details: the sport he loved, the car he wanted, the future he once planned.She laughs at his old jokes because she helped write them. He feels admired without effort. Understood without explanation. Soon, he is no longer messaging his ex. He is messaging the younger, adored version of himself she reflects back to him.

This is how the emotional affair with an ex unfolds:

> Past validation becomes present oxygen.
> Old intimacy becomes current temptation.
> Shared memories become private fantasies.

He tells himself it is not cheating. He's not meeting her. They're not touching. They're "just talking." But emotional infidelity begins not with bodies, *it begins with secrecy.*

The moment the messages are hidden, deleted, or minimized when the spouse walks into the room, the affair has already taken root. Staying in touch with an ex is rarely about the ex. It is about the part of the man that feels forgotten, and the woman who knows exactly how to make him feel remembered.

Online Emotional Intimacy: When Screens Become Safer Than Real Life

In the modern world, emotional cheating doesn't require a bar, a workplace, or a physical encounter. All it needs is an internet connection and someone who replies. What begins as harmless interactions—long chats on Instagram, conversations in gaming lobbies, private messages on apps, online forums, or hobby groups—can rapidly transform into a hidden relationship built on emotional gratification. Digital spaces feel innocent because there is no physical contact, yet they offer the most potent currency of all: attention, uninterrupted and tailored.

Online intimacy is seductive because it is curated. He speaks when he wants to. He ignores messages he doesn't like. He can be witty, confident, relaxed, and idealized.

There are no bills to argue about, no responsibilities, no criticisms, no domestic reality. Only selective vulnerability, his stress without his flaws, his dreams without his failures, his heart without accountability.

The woman on the other side experiences only the polished version of him, the version he wishes his partner saw. She becomes the witness to his best self, while his wife bears the weight of his tired, unfiltered self.

Long online conversations create false intimacy. Talking for hours about music, childhood trauma, mental health struggles, loneliness, or unfulfilled dreams becomes the emotional equivalent of undressing. There is a powerful psychological rush in being *heard* by someone who is not obligated to care. That rush becomes addictive. He begins to check his phone not for work or news, but for her messages. He goes to bed late replying to her and wakes up early to see if she texted back. The dopamine cycle takes hold: attention → anticipation → validation.

Online emotional cheating is uniquely dangerous because it feels "innocent." He will insist:

> "We've never met."
> "It's just a game."
> "She's just someone I talk to online."
> "You're overreacting."

But betrayal isn't defined by geography. It's defined by where the heart goes when it leaves the relationship.

When he shares his secrets with someone online instead of his spouse, when he runs to a stranger for comfort instead of his wife, when he deletes messages or clears chat logs, the affair has already begun. It doesn't matter that the connection is digital—what matters is that the emotional loyalty has migrated. Screens become the new bedroom. The keyboard becomes the mouth. The internet becomes an escape.

In the end, online intimacy and physical intimacy are not opposites—they are sequential. One is the seed; the other is the harvest.

Chapter 6

Seeking Admiration: The Ego's Affair

Some men do not cheat because they are lonely. They cheat because they crave admiration.

Attention becomes a drug—one that feeds the ego, not the heart. A passing smile, a flirtatious comment, a compliment on his shirt, a waitress who laughs at his jokes—suddenly he feels powerful again. Desired. Noticed. Relevant. For many men, admiration is not about wanting another woman; it is about wanting to feel like *someone worth wanting.*

In a long-term relationship, admiration often becomes quieter. Life gets busy. Bills, children, stress, routines. Compliments fade. Seduction becomes replaced by schedules. A wife may love him deeply, but the spark is buried under the weight of everyday obligations. He begins to feel invisible in his own home. Not criticized, not hated—simply *unseen.* And in that vulnerable state, the slightest attention from another woman feels like oxygen.

This is where dangerous thoughts begin:

She still thinks I'm attractive.
She thinks I'm interesting.
She respects me.
She sees something my wife no longer does.

He may never intend to cross a line physically. But emotional cheating is already underway the moment he becomes dependent on external admiration to feel whole. He starts dressing sharper for work, joking more with the barista, lingering longer with female coworkers, posting selfies online to see who reacts. Each like, each message, each flirt is a hit of dopamine telling him he still has value.

The problem isn't admiration; it is the pedestal. He uses these interactions to escape the ordinary version of himself: the man who pays bills, washes dishes, forgets to buy milk, disappoints someone, or feels inadequate. With other women, he gets to be the hero, the flirt, the charming guy with potential. He experiences himself through their eyes, not through the lens of his everyday responsibilities.

Men rarely understand this pattern as cheating because there is no sex involved. But admiration-seeking is *emotional infidelity in slow motion.* It is the prelude to every other form of betrayal.

Because one day, admiration will not be enough. The attention he enjoys will become attention he expects. He will chase it, cultivate it, and finally act on it. What begins as innocent validation often ends as an affair. Not because he truly loves the other woman, but because she makes him feel like someone worth loving.

Emotional Affairs Through Hobbies: When Shared Interests Become Shared Hearts

Not every affair begins with romance. Many begin with routine. A workout partner at the gym. A coworker you jog with every morning. A fishing companion who joins weekend trips. These relationships feel harmless because they are built around activities, not intimacy, yet they slowly become the places where emotional energy escapes the marriage. Hobbies offer something marriages often lose over time: enthusiasm. There is excitement in shared goals, improvement, and progress. When a man bonds with a woman over a hobby he is passionate about, she becomes associated with his best moments: his discipline, his growth, his confidence, his relief from stress. Instead of sharing those victories with his wife, he shares them with her.

It starts with casual encouragement:

"You're getting so much stronger."

"Wow, look how much you've improved."

"I'm proud of you."

Praise becomes admiration; admiration becomes connection. Soon, the woman who spots his bench press or sits beside him on the boat becomes the one who hears about his insecurities, work stress, fears, or dreams. What should be conversations with his partner at home become emotional confessions to someone who has no history of pain with him, only pleasure and progress. She sees him at his best, not his exhausted, irritated, distracted, or human moments. He feels known without resistance, validated without conflict, celebrated without obligation.

The danger of hobby-based emotional affairs is subtle. There is no candlelit dinner, no secret hotel room. It doesn't look like cheating, so no one questions it. He spends "just an extra hour" at the gym. He goes fishing early "because the weather is perfect." He stays to train "because she needed a partner."

These hours become an emotional investment. The wife begins to feel like the spectator of his life, while the hobby partner becomes the participant. The activity becomes the doorway to intimacy, not because of sex, but because of *shared meaning*. When he experiences joy, relief, improvement, or escape with another woman, she becomes the symbol of liberation, and his wife the symbol of responsibility.

This is how emotional affairs hide in plain sight: not in whispers or messages, but in smiles; long sessions; shared challenges; softball teams; yoga partners; running clubs; two people sweating, laughing, bonding, and telling themselves, "We're just training." But every repetition, every trip, every shared accomplishment is another brick in the wall that separates him from the person he pledged his life to. The affair doesn't start when he kisses her, it starts when he begins to *save his stories, victories, and fears for her instead of his wife.*

Chapter 8

Using a Female Friend as a Therapist: When Venting Becomes Betrayal

Emotional infidelity rarely begins with flirtation; it begins with confession. A man who feels misunderstood, nagged, overlooked, or unappreciated at home looks for someone who will not argue back, someone who will not challenge him, someone who will not remind him of his responsibilities. He finds a female friend who listens. It feels innocent, even therapeutic. She offers empathy, where his wife offers reality. She comforts, while his wife confronts. Her validation becomes the cure for the pain he refuses to address in his marriage.

At first, the conversations seem harmless. He vented about work, about stress, about small disappointments. But the human brain follows patterns: you return to the person who makes you feel safe. Safety soon transforms into dependency. Instead of talking to his wife, he texts the other woman. Instead of holding discomfort at home, he seeks relief elsewhere. Slowly, she becomes the emotional first responder.

She receives his frustrations, his fears, his doubts, his wounds. He is not sharing information; he is outsourcing intimacy.

A dangerous shift happens here. He stops telling his wife how he feels. He stops asking her to understand him. He stops trying to repair the conflict. He simply escapes the discomfort of the marriage by opening another emotional door. The wife becomes the person he hides from; the friend becomes the person he runs to.

Using a female friend like a therapist does not heal him. It reinforces his avoidance. He is praised without accountability. She validates his emotions without seeing his flaws, his laziness, his stubbornness, or his contributions to the conflict. She sees him only as the misunderstood victim. And he willingly accepts that role because it feels good. In her eyes, he is the hero of a painful story. At home, he might feel like the problem.

A wife shares the stress of real life: children, finances, chores, expectations, and workload. A female friend shares none of it. She watches from a distance, untouched by responsibility, unburdened by history. She has the luxury of admiration because she has no obligation to reality. He never has to see how she would behave in a long-term relationship. He gets her best version. She gets his wounded version. His wife gets whatever is left.

There is an especially corrosive moment in this pattern: he begins to compare the two women. Not consciously at first, but emotionally. She listens, his wife argues. She validates, his wife questions. She supports, his wife challenges. He convinces himself he has found someone who "gets him," someone who "accepts him," someone who "treats him better." This is how emotional affairs rewrite identity: they turn empathy into superiority.

The betrayal becomes deeper when he starts speaking about his wife to the other woman. He shares her flaws, her mistakes, her bad moods, her insecurities. He treats his partner like a case file, and the new woman becomes the judge. Every negative story he tells her makes her feel closer to him. Every complaint becomes intimacy. He may think he is releasing pressure, but he is poisoning the foundation of his marriage. A relationship cannot survive when its wounds are discussed with outsiders instead of addressed within.

The emotional replacement becomes complete when she becomes his first thought—not the wife he married, but the woman he vents to. He texts her before he tells his spouse. He hears her voice in his head during arguments. He anticipates her comfort before facing conflict.

This is infidelity in its purest emotional form. It is a disloyalty of trust. It is abandonment of vulnerability. It is taking the most private parts of the marriage and placing them in someone else's hands.

Many men say, "We never had sex." They cling to that phrase as if it absolves them. But infidelity does not begin with bodies; it begins with secrets. The moment he shares his heart somewhere else, he has cheated, because he has denied his partner the chance to understand him, to repair with him, to grow alongside him.

Marriage is not destroyed by silence. It is destroyed by the voices invited in to replace it.

Chapter 9

Love-Bombing Another Woman: Compliments, Gifts, Emotional Idealization, and the Fantasy Future

Love-bombing is not love.

It is an emotional strategy, often unconscious, that floods another woman with admiration, praise, intensity, and promises until she feels chosen in a way his wife no longer does. It is the performance of romance without responsibility. The man paints her as extraordinary, special, exceptional. He lavishes compliments like confetti, sends late-night messages, buys thoughtful gifts, and speaks to her as if she is the missing piece of his soul. The attention is intoxicating for both of them.

Love-bombing does not emerge from abundance; it emerges from emotional deprivation. When a man feels unappreciated, unseen, or dulled by routine, he chases the feeling of being desirable. The woman who receives the love-bombing becomes a reflection of who he wants to be, rather than who he actually is. He idealizes her because it allows him to idealize himself. He treats her as a fantasy, a clean slate untouched by arguments, chores, history, or exhaustion. She does not know the tired father, the impatient spouse, or the flawed human being. She knows the upgraded version of him: the romantic, the attentive man, the dreamer.

Love-bombing is powerful because it bypasses reality and goes straight to imagination. He tells her how beautiful she is, how wise, how misunderstood, how special, not because he has discovered something profound, but because she listens without challenging him. He feeds her emotional hunger while she feeds his ego. He might say, "I've never felt this way before," "You deserve someone who sees you," or "If I had met you sooner, everything would have been different." These statements are not expressions of truth; they are invitations into a parallel life where consequences do not exist.

The gifts and compliments are not acts of generosity. They are emotional anchors. The flowers, the surprise coffee, the thoughtful text at midnight, each one quietly says, "I am investing in you instead of my wife." The woman begins to feel uniquely chosen, valued above other people in his life. She is not just another person; she is "the one who understands him," "the one who listens," "the one he confides in." Slowly, she becomes the emotional center of his identity.

As the idealization intensifies, the relationship transitions from flirtation to *future-casting*. He speaks in promises. Not small promises, but cinematic ones:

> "We should travel together."
> "Someday I'll leave everything behind."
> "You're the type of woman a man could build a life with."

This is the most seductive stage of emotional cheating: he is not offering affection — he is offering possibility.

In his mind, the fantasy is easier than the marriage because it contains no history and no accountability. He does not remember the woman who stayed up at 2 a.m. with sick children; he remembers the girl who laughed at his jokes in college. He does not see the wife who pays bills, compromises, sacrifices, and forgives; He sees the flirtatious coworker who thinks he is brilliant. Fantasy is always more attractive than reality because it has no cost.

The tragedy is that love-bombing feels like destiny to the woman receiving it. She feels adored, pursued, emotionally fed. She confuses dopamine with devotion. What she is experiencing is not love; it is the relief of attention.

To the wife, the signs are subtle but unmistakable. He becomes distant at home but overly generous elsewhere. He becomes short-tempered with her but poetic with another woman. He stops trying in the relationship because he is alive somewhere else, in the fantasy he is creating.

Many men tell themselves they are simply being kind. They insist there is no betrayal because there is no physical act. But emotional cheating does not require skin.; It requires misplaced energy.

When he gives another woman the version of himself he once gave his wife—the flattery, the admiration, the excitement, the hope—he has already cheated. Not with his body, but with his future.

Chapter 10

Secret "Platonic" Friendships

A man does not need a hotel room or a sexual encounter to betray his marriage. Sometimes, all it takes is a friendship he protects from the light. A secret platonic friendship is not defined by sex—it is defined by *the parts of himself he reserves for another woman*. He knows it appears harmless on paper. They do not touch. They do not kiss. They do not meet in a bedroom. Yet he tells his wife nothing about her, or he downplays their connection, or he insists she is "just a friend." Justification becomes the shield, secrecy becomes the sin.

The danger is not that he has a female friend. Healthy marriages can withstand friendships with the opposite sex when boundaries, transparency, and respect remain intact. The danger is that he has a *private friendship*, one built on emotional intimacy, personal disclosure, and selective access to his inner world. He tells this woman things he does not tell his wife. He laughs with her in a way he no longer laughs at home. He shares his disappointments, frustrations, and dreams. She becomes the one who validates him. That validation becomes addictive.

A secret emotional companion creates a split reality. In one life, he is the partner, parent, provider, and responsible adult; in the other, he is carefree, charming, desirable, interesting, and admired. The "friend" receives the curated version of him, the highlight reel without his exhaustion, flaws, failures, or everyday burdens. His wife gets the unfiltered version: the man who forgets things, who struggles, who is tired, who sometimes disappoints. The more he hides, the more he invests, and the more he invests, the more he must hide.

A platonic friendship becomes an emotional affair the moment it requires secrecy to survive. He deletes messages. He changes contact names. He avoids talking about her. He silences notifications. He insists, "You're overreacting" when questioned.

These behaviors are not neutral. They are defensive. They reveal that he knows something is crossing a boundary—otherwise, there would be nothing to hide.

Even the way he frames her is telling. He does not say "she's a colleague" **or** "we're in the same group"; he says "you're being dramatic," "you're insecure," or "you're crazy." He shifts the attention away from the behavior and onto his wife's reaction. This is how emotional affairs protect themselves: they make the betrayed partner feel irrational instead of the betrayer feeling accountable.

Secret friendships with the opposite sex often become more powerful than physical affairs because they carry the illusion of innocence. There is no physical violation, so the man tells himself he has done nothing wrong. Yet he has already redirected emotional loyalty. He shares his victories, his fears, and his hurts with someone who did not walk through life with him. He allows another woman to become his comfort, his support, his refuge. He gives her the quality of attention that belongs only to his spouse.

The most dangerous part of emotional affairs is that they feel righteous. He tells himself:

She listens.
She understands.
She cares.
My wife doesn't.

He forgets that the wife is burdened with the weight of real life, and the "friend" is burdened with nothing. The friend receives the glow of him, the idealized version, the man who tries. The wife holds the truth of him, the man who fails, the man who gets tired, the man who is human.

Secret friendships are not "just friendships." They are *rehearsals for infidelity.* And the moment he begins protecting the relationship from view, he has already stepped outside the marriage—even if his body never left the home.

Chapter 11

Transactional Sex: Escorts, Massage Parlors, and the Illusion of No Emotional Consequences

Transactional sex is infidelity stripped of romance and layered with denial. It is the decision to pay for a sexual experience—through escorts, massage parlors, "happy endings," online platforms, or discreet services—with the belief that money sterilizes the betrayal. The man tells himself, "It isn't emotional," "It doesn't mean anything," "She's not important," "It's just a release." He hides behind the idea that because there is no emotional attachment, there is no true cheating. But the absence of feelings does not erase the breach of trust. Masculine desire does not justify breaking vows.

Men who seek transactional sex often do so because it feels controlled, predictable, and consequence-free. There is no risk of rejection, no effort to impress, no emotional vulnerability, and no accountability. He pays for attention, pleasure, and validation in the most primitive form. For one hour, he can pretend he is desired, powerful, and free from the expectations of partnership. The transaction becomes a temporary escape from the reality of everyday life, a moment in which he gets to exist without judgment, without disappointment, and without responsibility.

But transactional sex carries its own psychological dangers. It reinforces the belief that intimacy is something to be consumed rather than cultivated. He learns to disconnect sex from connection, partner from pleasure, loyalty from satisfaction. The wife becomes a figure in his domestic life— mother, homemaker, roommate, administrator— while the prostitute or masseuse becomes the vessel of indulgence. He compartmentalizes his humanity. One part of him is a husband; the other part lives in the shadows and pretends he does not owe anyone honesty.

This form of cheating is often justified through the language of minimization:

> "It's just physical."
> "It's not emotional."
> "She's not a real person to me."
> "It doesn't affect the marriage."

In reality, transactional sex is rooted in emotional avoidance. He would not need to outsource intimacy if he were capable of addressing the emotional wounds inside the relationship. He buys relief because he lacks courage. He pays for pleasure because he will not face his partner's disappointment. He gambles trust because he refuses vulnerability. Infidelity through money is not an escape from consequences; it is a shortcut to them.

The impact on the spouse is profound and uniquely brutal. It is not simply that he touched another body. It is that he risked her health, her dignity, and her sense of safety without her consent. She begins to question every physical interaction they ever shared. Did he come home after touching another woman? Did he lie in her bed while carrying the scent of betrayal? Did he protect himself? Was she exposed? The damage is not philosophical; it is visceral.

Even the man who believes he is not emotionally invested in the encounter fails to recognize the emotional investment in the decision. He is emotionally invested in not feeling judged. He is emotionally invested in the illusion of control. He is emotionally invested in being desired without having to earn it. That emotional currency is simply being exchanged for cash.

Transactional sex is not "just sex." It is the commodification of intimacy, the separation of body from trust, and the deliberate circumvention of moral responsibility. It is the moment a man decides that loyalty is optional, honesty is inconvenient, and pleasure is more valuable than integrity. Whether it lasts fifteen minutes or a night, whether it happens once or a hundred times, it is infidelity. And unlike emotional betrayal, it invites strangers directly into the most sacred space of the marriage: the body.

Chapter 12

One-Night Stands: Bars, Trips, Bachelor Weekends, and Conferences

One-night stands are the form of infidelity most often disguised as "a mistake," a moment of weakness, or alcohol-fueled stupidity. They happen in hotel rooms, at conferences, on business trips, during bachelor parties, or after nights out with friends. The environment is designed for impulsiveness: anonymity, alcohol, secrecy, and distance from routine. The man convinces himself that what happens "away from home" is separate from the life he returns to. He believes that if there is no emotional connection, there is no real betrayal. The simplicity makes it easier to excuse, but the impact is no less catastrophic.

The most seductive characteristic of the one-night stand is *the absence of continuity*. There is no texting, no courting, no months of emotional grooming. There is only the moment: lust, adrenaline, opportunity. He tells himself it "just happened." Yet there is always a chain of micro-decisions that lead to it: staying for another drink, flirting with the stranger at the bar, exchanging jokes, agreeing to leave together, closing the hotel door. A one-night stand is not an accident. It is a series of choices made in silence.

For many men, one-night stands are not about attraction to another woman; they are about escape. Escape from stress, from responsibility, from feeling unappreciated, from feeling old, from feeling irrelevant. The bar, the party, or the work trip becomes a portal to a different version of himself—younger, funnier, reckless, impulsive. He pursues sex not because of who she is, but because of how *he* feels in her presence: uninhibited, exciting, alive.

The moment of betrayal is often brief but rich in fantasy. He does not have to be a husband. He does not have to be a father. He does not have to be a provider or a responsible man. He can be the attractive stranger, the charming traveler, the confident party-goer. The woman he sleeps with becomes a temporary witness to a version of himself that reality no longer reflects.

But when one-night stands end, the reckoning begins. The sexual partner vanishes, but the consequences do not. He returns home with secrets tucked into his brain like poison capsules. He hugs his wife, drives his children to school, returns to work, and pretends his body didn't betray everyone who loves him. The lie becomes heavier with every normal task. He becomes hyper-paranoid, resentful, detached, or overly affectionate, not because of love, but because of guilt.

The betrayed partner often suffers the worst psychological torture from these encounters:

> "How many times?"
> "With whom?"
> "Was it better than with me?"
> "Did he think about her afterward?"
> "Was I on his mind at all?"

One-night stands attack the most primal part of intimacy: sexual exclusivity. They reduce the marriage bed to a shared commodity and destroy the safety that partners expect from one another. Even if the event was impulsive, the impact is permanent: the moment he crosses that line, the relationship is no longer what it was before.

People often defend one-night stands by claiming there were no feelings involved. But infidelity is not measured by emotion. It is measured by betrayal. The man who chooses a stranger's body over his wife's loyalty has not made a "minor" mistake; he has placed lust above respect, impulse above integrity, and momentary pleasure above the sanctity of his relationship.

A one-night stand may last only an hour, but it leaves a stain that can last a lifetime.

Chapter 13

Sugar Arrangements: Financial Support in Exchange for Intimacy

Sugar arrangements represent a particularly insidious form of infidelity because they combine sex, power, fantasy, and money into a single transaction. Unlike one-night stands, which often masquerade as impulsive mistakes, sugar relationships are structured, negotiated, and intentional. The man enters into an agreement: he provides financial support, and she provides intimacy—emotional, sexual, or both. It is not a misunderstanding. It is a contract of betrayal.

Sugar dynamics are seductive because they offer the illusion of control. He tells himself he is not cheating—he is "helping," "sponsoring," or "mentoring." He disguises his desire as generosity. He rationalizes it:

> "She needs stability."
> "She's young and struggling."
> "I'm providing opportunities."

In truth, he is buying youth, admiration, attention, and sex with the currency of his wallet. He gets to feel powerful, desired, and chosen. He becomes the savior, the benefactor, the mentor—roles that protect his ego and bypass accountability.

Sugar relationships allow a man to create an alternate life with no consequences. He does not need to impress through personality, character, or growth. He can simply pay his way into intimacy. The dynamics are transactional, yet emotionally disguised: dinners, vacations, designer gifts, shopping allowances, rent payments, business investments. The relationship becomes a curated fantasy, one where he is interesting, admired, and valuable simply because he funds another woman's lifestyle.

In a marriage, intimacy is the result of shared sacrifice, vulnerability, compromise, forgiveness, and history; in a sugar arrangement, intimacy is a reward. He gets affection for attention, sex for sponsorship, and validation for money. It is intimacy without responsibility. This is why men find it intoxicating. They do not need to confront their own emotional shortcomings. They only need to open their wallet.

The psychological danger is in the *power imbalance*. The woman becomes dependent on his money; he becomes dependent on her admiration. He begins to believe that he is more valued by her than by his wife—not because he is a better man, but because *he is a better provider*. It is a fragile illusion. The moment the payments stop, so does the affection. He mistakes financial leverage for romantic worth.

Sugar relationships are not free from emotion. They create identity wounds on both sides. The man begins to feel entitled to sexual attention because he has paid for it. The woman begins to feel obligated to provide it because she has accepted help. The intimacy becomes a debt: owed, traded, repeated.

And in the background sits the spouse, unaware that the family's resources, emotional energy, and loyalty are being diverted into another person's lifestyle. She does not know that the vacations, gifts, or private dinners she imagined sharing were given to someone who has earned nothing but willingness. The betrayal is not only sexual; it is economic. He invests marital wealth in the destruction of the marriage itself.

Some men convince themselves it is safer because there is no emotional attachment. But sugar arrangements often produce *deeper emotional corruption* than an affair of passion. They replace love with transaction, intimacy with leverage, loyalty with access. They teach men to see women as commodities, disposable, purchasable, replaceable.

The devastating truth is simple: sugar arrangements are not relationships at all. They are *contracts designed to mimic intimacy* for a price. And when a husband pays another woman for closeness, admiration, or sex, he is not just cheating on his wife; he is erasing the very meaning of intimacy itself.

Chapter 14

Porn Addiction Replacing Intimacy: Compulsive Use, Cam Models, and Live Chat

Pornography is often dismissed as "harmless"—a private habit, a stress release, something every man does. But when it becomes compulsive, consuming hours of thought, time, and energy, it becomes a silent form of infidelity. Porn addiction is not just about watching sexual content. It is about replacing emotional and physical intimacy with a digital substitute that asks for nothing in return. The screen becomes the lover, the escape, the place he goes to feel stimulated without vulnerability, effort, or accountability.

Porn addiction rewires the brain the same way substance addiction does. It floods dopamine into the nervous system, creating an artificial high that real intimacy cannot compete with. The body learns to respond to novelty over connection, pixels over partnership. The spouse becomes familiar, predictable, real. Porn offers endless variety, impossibly perfect bodies, unrealistic sexual scenarios, and fantasies that require no communication, consent, or emotional investment. He does not have to show up as a partner. He only needs to exist as an observer.

The danger grows when porn evolves into interactive sex: cam models, live chat rooms, OnlyFans subscriptions, private Snapchats. These platforms blur the line between fantasy and reality. He can message performers, request actions, receive attention tailored to his desires. The interaction is transactional: payment in exchange for sexual performance, validation, attention. The addiction deepens because now, rather than observing from afar, he becomes a participant. He is no longer just watching pornography; he is *in a relationship with it.*

The wife begins to feel like she is competing with ghosts. She cannot know the countless bodies, scenarios, or fantasies he has consumed. She only feels the withdrawal. Less affection, less patience, less desire, less presence. Sex becomes mechanical, pressured, or avoided entirely. He prefers the control of the screen—where he can fast-forward, skip, mute, or close a tab—over the vulnerability of real intimacy, where he must communicate, show empathy, and confront his own insecurities.

Porn addiction often becomes a cycle of shame. He hides his habits, lies about it, erases browser history, uses incognito mode, watches in bathrooms or late at night, sneaks into guest rooms, or claims exhaustion. He promises to stop, then relapses. The addiction thrives in secrecy and guilt, both of which pull him further away from his spouse. The more he escapes into porn, the less capable he becomes of experiencing authentic sexual connection. He begins to demand porn-like performance in real life. The wife becomes inadequate, boring, not enough. The problem is not her body; it is his brain.

Wives often experience porn addiction as betrayal because it replaces them without their consent. They feel rejected, compared, humiliated, unwanted. The intimacy of marriage becomes secondary to the fantasy of strangers. The husband is in the same room but mentally gone, sexually elsewhere. It is not "just porn"; it is the erosion of erotic love. It trains him to respond to stimulation rather than connection, to novelty rather than loyalty, to pixels rather than partnership.

Porn becomes the third person in the marriage: silent, tireless, always available, never arguing. It demands nothing but attention and rewards him with dopamine every time. He believes he is free because there is no other woman involved. In truth, he has replaced his wife with a digital harem. When pornography becomes the primary outlet for sexual desire, marriage stops being a place of intimacy and becomes a place of emotional loneliness. The addiction wins not by seduction, but by gradual replacement.

Porn addiction is a betrayal not because a man touches another body, but because he withdraws his own. He abandons his partner in the most intimate dimension of the relationship. He gives his mind, his sexuality, and his fantasies to an industry built on illusion and exploitation. And the tragic irony is that the more he consumes it, the less he can love the person he promised his body to, because he no longer knows how to be present within real intimacy.

Chapter 15

Sexual Texting or Sexting: Photos, Videos, and Digital Sexuality

Sexting is not accidental. It is deliberate, chosen, and deeply intimate. When a man begins sending sexual messages, explicit photos, or videos to another woman, he is crossing one of the clearest and most undeniable boundaries of fidelity. It is not "just texting." It is the digital equivalent of undressing in front of someone else. Words become hands. Images become skin. Messages become bodies touching in the imagination.

Sexting is powerful because it bypasses the obstacles that come with real-life physical affairs. There is no scheduling, no hotel rooms, no witnesses, no logistics. Just a phone and a willing partner. Technology gives the illusion of safety. He can send a picture, delete the conversation, close the app, and pretend nothing happened. He convinces himself it is harmless because it lacks physical contact. In truth, it is a form of cheating that often feels more exciting than sex because it comes packaged in secrecy, novelty, anticipation, and the intoxication of being desired.

It begins like emotional texting: compliments, flirtation, attention. Then one message crosses the line: a provocative joke, a sexual comment, a late-night selfie. He waits for her reaction. If she plays along, the game begins. The sexual tension escalates, the emojis change, the tone shifts. Soon, he sends pictures he would never want his wife to see and types words he would never dare say to her. The phone becomes a bedroom he carries everywhere.

Sexting is addictive because it turns intimacy into instant gratification:

> He can receive desire on demand.
> He can rewind a compliment by rereading it.
> He can rewatch a video.
> He can create fantasy versions of himself without ever being vulnerable in real life.

Unlike emotional cheating, which builds slowly, sexting escalates like a fire. Every message raises the stakes. Every reply invites bolder content. Every image becomes a promise: "I want you."

What many men fail to understand is that sexting is not just erotic expression; it is *emotional exposure*. He gives another woman access to his desires, his body, and the most private dimension of his sexuality. He begins to crave her reaction more than real intimacy with his spouse. Even if he has sex at home, the most intense part of him, the hungry, impulsive, youthful, daring part, is now reserved for someone else. His wife becomes the partner of obligation. The sexting partner becomes the partner of excitement.

For the betrayed spouse, sexting is often more painful than physical infidelity:

She sees screenshots, not guesses.
She sees what he typed, not what she imagines.
She sees photos he took for someone else: poses, angles, underwear, erections, shaved areas, body parts he never presented for her.

It forces her to confront a brutal reality: *another woman was invited into the intimate world that used to belong to her alone.*
Men often defend sexting by saying:

"We never met."
"It was only fantasy."
"It was just words."

These justifications miss the truth: Sexting is not a mistake; it is a *decision to betray in the mind, the imagination, and the body.* The absence of intercourse does not absolve the emotional and sexual betrayal. The mind is the first organ that cheats. The phone is simply the tool that makes it visible.

When a man sends sexual content to another woman, he is not just touching his phone—he is touching her with his intention. The moment he types, "Send me more," the relationship is no longer digital. It is physical desire—outsourced and digitized—destroying the intimacy that once lived in his marriage.

Chapter 16

Workplace Sex: When Professional Proximity Turns Into Physical Betrayal

Workplace sex is one of the most devastating forms of infidelity because it grows in the place where a man spends most of his waking life. It does not happen in a random bar or on a reckless trip. It happens in conference rooms, hotel lobbies, quiet offices after hours, elevators, business trips, and company retreats. The emotional seeds are planted long before the physical act. Two people share deadlines, pressure, victories, frustrations, jokes, travel, and long hours in environments where loyalty to family is a distant thought and performance, ambition, and recognition dominate.

The affair begins under fluorescent lights, not candlelit dinners. Late projects lead to takeout meals. Quick conversations lead to private jokes. After-work drinks lead to confessions:

"My marriage is complicated."

"We're more like roommates."

"She just doesn't understand me."

The woman becomes a colleague first, a confidante second, and eventually an emotional partner. Sex arrives as *the final step*, not the beginning. By the time bodies meet, the boundaries have been crossed repeatedly in the mind.

Workplace sex is uniquely dangerous because it offers *constant access*. Unlike a fling or a stranger, the affair partner is woven into his daily life. He sees her every day. They exchange glances as they pass in the hallway. Meetings become foreplay. Lunch breaks become secrets. Team trips become opportunities. Real life becomes a rehearsal until a hotel door finally closes behind them.

The most seductive ingredient is familiarity. He does not need to impress her. She has already seen him frustrated at meetings, struggling with tasks, joking with coworkers. She knows his temperament, his strengths, his weaknesses. He believes she understands him in a way his wife does not. He confuses professional compatibility with romantic destiny.

Workplace sex often feels risk-free to the betrayer: no dating apps, no escort websites, no travel for nightlife. It is hidden in the normalcy of everyday life. Nobody questions why he is texting her. Nobody thinks twice when they travel together. Nobody suspects that behind the business attire and spreadsheets are stolen kisses, bathroom encounters, and bodies pressed against hotel walls.

The betrayal is profound for the spouse because it infects every corner of her husband's life. She is not only betrayed in the home; she is betrayed in his professional world. He returns from work carrying the scent of another woman. He leaves the house not to provide or advance his career, but to seek the company of someone he has chosen over his vows. His job—the place she respects, encourages, and supports—becomes the arena of betrayal.

Workplace sex is not about lack of opportunity; it is about deliberate risk. The thrill is magnified by danger: the possibility of getting caught, the taboo of the location, the adrenaline of the forbidden. The secrecy becomes erotic. The stolen time becomes a high. He begins to live two lives: the face he wears at home and the body he shares at work.

When exposed, workplace affairs often produce the most catastrophic collapse. He cannot easily separate from the other woman without changing jobs or enduring ongoing proximity: coworkers know, rumors spread, supervisors intervene. He may lose his position, his reputation, and his career—all in pursuit of lust disguised as connection.

Workplace sex is often justified with the same lines:

> "It just happened."
> "We were drunk."
> "It was a bad night."

But the truth is more brutal: it did not *just happen*. It was built through every private meeting, every shared ride, every hidden message, every unchallenged flirtation.

When a man gives his body to someone at work, he contaminates the very environment that feeds his family. He risks his marriage, his integrity, his livelihood, and his dignity. All in exchange for a moment where impulse ruled over responsibility.

It is not simply physical betrayal. It is the destruction of the life he built from the inside out.

Chapter 17

Sex Tourism: "Out of Town" as an Excuse for No Consequences

Sex tourism is one of the most deliberate and premeditated forms of infidelity. It is not an accident, not a drunken mistake, not a moment of weakness. It is a choice made with full intention: traveling to a location where sexual encounters are easily accessible, widely normalized, and detached from moral consequence. These environments are specifically designed to blur responsibility. Bars in foreign countries, beach resorts, brothels overseas, red-light districts, exotic massage parlors, cruise ships, bachelor destinations. The unspoken message is: "What happens here doesn't count."

The psychology behind sex tourism is rooted in anonymity. At home, a man is a husband, a father, a coworker, a respectable member of society. Abroad, he becomes a ghost. No neighbors, no friends, no colleagues, no reputation. His identity dissolves into the crowd. He believes he can buy intimacy, use bodies, and disappear without consequence. The distance between his actions and his life gives him permission to abandon his values. He cheats because he believes he will not be caught, not because he is desperate for love.

Many men who engage in sex tourism convince themselves they are doing something "culturally normal." They cite bachelor parties, business trips, conference after-parties, or nights on foreign beaches as an excuse. They claim, "Everyone does it there," or "It's not cheating, it's just the culture." But every foreign bed is a betrayal of the home they return to. Every paid encounter is a declaration that fidelity is conditional—valid only when convenient.

Sex tourism is especially dangerous because it often involves *exploitation and power imbalances*. The "other woman" is rarely a romantic partner. She may be a sex worker living in poverty, a trafficked minor, or someone forced into the industry by economic desperation. The cheater converts his money into permission, unconscious of the fact that he is not only betraying his spouse, he is participating in global human suffering. Infidelity here is not just a moral failure—it is a form of predatory consumption.

The mentality is chillingly simple: "It doesn't count if it happens away from home."

He convinces himself that physical distance equals emotional distance. That the wife will never know. That the marriage stays untouched. But the body remembers. The mind remembers. He carries the betrayal back with him: through airports, through customs, through the front door. He lies with his passport in his pocket and guilt in his bloodstream.

When the truth emerges, the spouse experiences a particular kind of agony. It is not just the betrayal of sex; it is the betrayal of intentionality. He *planned* to have sex with someone else. He traveled for it. He paid for it. He scheduled it into his life. It was not impulsive. It was calculated. She realizes she was not momentarily replaced; she was deliberately abandoned.

Sex tourism corrupts the meaning of intimacy in the worst way.

It transforms sex into a recreational activity, something purchased, consumed, and discarded. It teaches the man to view fidelity as optional, geographic, and negotiable. It plants the belief that marriage is sacred only within a zip code, and meaningless on a foreign street.

This is not "boys being boys." This is not "just how things are overseas." Sex tourism is the decision to leave loyalty behind at the airport and reclaim it only when returning home. It is cowardice disguised as adventure, selfishness disguised as culture, and betrayal disguised as freedom.

Chapter 18

Micro-Cheating in Person: Grabbing, Touching, and Grinding at Clubs

Micro-cheating is the gateway drug of infidelity. It is the physical flirtation a man engages in when he wants the thrill of being desired without the accountability of calling it cheating. This is the hand on a stranger's waist at a bar, the "accidental" brush of fingers on the lower back, the slow dance pressed against someone's body at a club, the playful grabbing on the dance floor when the music is loud and the lights are low. It is the moment the body crosses a line the mouth refuses to admit.

Unlike emotional affairs or planned sexual encounters, micro-cheating happens in environments built for impulsiveness: bars, clubs, concerts, bachelor parties, nightlife trips, crowded events. Alcohol blurs judgment, peer pressure provides permission, and bodies are close enough to pretend the intimacy "just happened." He gets to touch someone else and tells himself it's harmless because there was no exchange of numbers, no sexual act, no relationship. But physical boundaries are not measured by intercourse; they are measured by *intent*.

Micro-cheating exists in the gray zone of betrayal. It is subtle. It is deniable. It is designed to be forgettable. He can say, "It didn't mean anything," "It was just a dance," or "We were just messing around." He may never even learn the woman's name. But the purpose was clear: he wanted to feel desired by someone who was not his spouse. He wanted to taste the thrill of being wanted in public while pretending it was nothing in private.

Many men's first excuse is to claim it's "just physical fun." They treat touching as recreational and flirting as a sport. But micro-cheating is a declaration of unmet desire seeking nourishment outside the marriage. It is not about the stranger; it is about the ego. The wife becomes invisible in the room. Her role fades from lover to spectator. He leaves the marriage emotionally to experience attention that requires no responsibility.

The damage is not in the seconds of contact; it is in the *message* the contact sends. A husband who grinds against another woman or grabs her waist is not confused. He is using another body as an instrument of validation. That act says, "I want pleasure without consequences." It says, "I'm willing to put my marriage at risk for a moment of ego." It says, "I prefer the heat of strangers over the intimacy I built with my wife."

Micro-cheating is especially dangerous because it often escalates. A hand on the hip becomes a hand on the thigh. A dance becomes a kiss. A kiss becomes a phone number. A phone number becomes a night together. Infidelity is rarely born from grand passion; it is born from *small permissions* repeated until they become habits.

And when a wife discovers this kind of betrayal, the pain is unique. She realizes that her husband's fidelity is fragile, not broken by emotional attachment or long-term planning, but shattered by the first attractive body that passes him in a crowded room. She is forced to confront the truth: He didn't need to love someone else to betray her. He only needed an opportunity.

Micro-cheating is not harmless. It is not "boys being boys." It is not "just dancing." It is the physical expression of emotional disloyalty, the rehearsal for bigger betrayals, and the moment a man chooses his impulses over his integrity.

Chapter 19

Using Dating Apps: "Just Browsing," Swiping, Talking, and Hooking Up

Dating apps have become one of the most deceptive forms of infidelity because they disguise betrayal as curiosity. A married man downloads Tinder, Bumble, Hinge, Plenty of Fish, or even niche "sugar dating" apps and tells himself he is "just looking." He claims he is swiping out of boredom, ego, validation, or entertainment. But every swipe is a statement of intent. You do not visit a marketplace unless you are willing to browse the merchandise. And you do not browse merchandise unless you are willing to buy.

The slippery slope begins with anonymity. Behind a username, profile picture, and vague bio, he is no longer a husband. He becomes a single man. He gets to rewrite his identity: choosing what to reveal, what to hide, and how to present himself. He posts pictures that make him look attractive, interesting, fit, and successful. He becomes a polished version of himself, selling a fantasy of availability.

The marriage disappears in a few taps, replaced by adrenaline and opportunity:

"Just browsing" eventually becomes messaging.
Messaging becomes flirting.
Flirting becomes meeting.
Meeting becomes sex.

It is not a sudden fall. It is a controlled descent — a staircase of micro-decisions he knows he should not take, each one justified by denial.

Dating apps are uniquely dangerous because they *gamify infidelity*. The brain treats swiping like a slot machine: one rejection, two rejections, then a match, dopamine hits, ego expands. He begins to measure his worth not by loyalty or integrity, but by how many women swipe right on him. Every match becomes proof that he "still has it." Every flirtation becomes oxygen for the parts of him that feel neglected at home.

From the outside, it looks like harmless digital exploration. From the inside, it is the emotional equivalent of walking into a hotel room and closing the blinds. Even if he never meets anyone in person, he has already broken the psychological contract of fidelity. He has made himself available to strangers: emotionally, sexually, and sometimes physically.

Some men escalate further. They create fake profiles. They use secret email addresses. They switch their relationship status to "single." They hide rings from photos. They travel to other cities "for work" to meet matches. They use disappearing-message apps, burner numbers, Snapchat, Telegram, Whisper. They enter the world of infidelity with the full intention of leaving no trace.

When the betrayed spouse discovers this, she experiences a unique kind of heartbreak. She does not just confront a single affair. She confronts *thousands of potential affairs* he invited into his life. Every swipe is a question mark:

> "Was he planning to meet her?"
> "Did they talk?"
> "Did they go out?"
> "Did they sleep together?"

The pain is exponential because the betrayal is not with one person; it is with dozens, maybe hundreds.

Men often defend dating apps with weak excuses:

> "I never met anyone."
> "I was just curious."
> "It was just fun."

But apps are not toys. They are marketplaces built for connection, desire, and sex. You do not wander into a bank for fun, or look at rental listings if you are not thinking of moving. When a man joins a dating app while married, he is not exploring; he is preparing.

Infidelity is not defined by whether he crossed the finish line. It is defined by whether he entered the race. The moment he installs an app, uploads photos, writes a bio, and starts swiping, he has already left the marriage in search of the next possibility.

Part II

How Women Cheat on Men

Emotional Ways

Chapter 20   Emotional Replacement: Women Forming a Deep
Connection With a Man Who Listens and
Validates Her   58

Chapter 21   Fantasy Relationship: Imagining a Life With
Someone Else, Romantic Daydreaming   61

Chapter 22   Affair of the Heart With a Coworker: Sharing
Details She Denies Her Husband   65

Chapter 23   Reconnecting With an Old Flame: Nostalgia,
Messages, "I Wonder What Could've Been."   70

Chapter 24   Validation From Compliments: Living on
Attention From Male Friends or Strangers   74

Chapter 25   Venting to Another Man About Her Marriage:
Emotional Betrayal Disguised as Friendship   78

Chapter 26   The "Work Husband" or Gym Partner: Comfort,
Partnership, Inside Jokes, and the Disappearance
of Boundaries   82

Chapter 27   Posting Seductive Photos: Not for Her Husband,
              but for Other Men   87

Chapter 28   Online Emotional Bonds: DMs, Comments, and
              Long Digital Relationships   92

Chapter 29   Secret Friendships: Hiding Them Because She
              Knows Her Husband Wouldn't Approve   97

Sexual Ways

Chapter 30   Physical Affair: Sexual Encounters With
              Someone Else   101

Chapter 31   Revenge Sex: Cheating Because She Felt Betrayed,
              Neglected, or Hurt   106

Chapter 32   Sexual Texting and Photos: Sending Nudes,
              Sexting, and Explicit Messages   110

Chapter 33   Affairs With "Safe" Male Friends: The Guy She
              Insists Is "Just a Friend"   115

Chapter 34   Sex During Business Trips: Conferences, Retreats,
              and Vacations With Friends   117

Chapter 35   Hookups With Exes: Comfortable, Familiar
              With Low Emotional Risk   120

Chapter 36   Sex for Validation: Using Intimacy to Feel
              Wanted, Powerful, and Admired   123

Chapter 37   Digital Escorts/Cam Interactions: Paying or
              Receiving Sexual Attention Online   126

Chapter 38   Club Hookups: Kissing, Touching, Grinding, and
              Sexual Contact in Nightlife Settings   129

Chapter 39   Using Dating Apps: "Just Talking," Curiosity,
              Flirting, Then Progressing to Sex   132

Epilogue   The Roads Back to Ourselves   135

Chapter 20

Emotional Replacement: Women Forming a Deep Connection With a Man Who Listens and Validates Her

Women rarely begin cheating with their bodies. They begin with their hearts. The first step is not sex, but *emotional substitution*, giving another man the role her husband once held. Instead of confiding in her partner, she begins confiding in someone else. Instead of seeking comfort at home, she seeks it in this new presence. The emotional intimacy is not accidental; it is carefully grown through conversations, empathy, consistency, and attention.

It starts innocently: a co-worker, a gym partner, a neighbor, someone in her social circle, or even a stranger online. He laughs at her jokes. He listens without interrupting. He remembers details her husband forgets. He notices when she changes her hair, when she looks tired, when she seems overwhelmed. His attention feels like validation, his compliments feel like oxygen. She tells herself she is only talking to someone who "gets it."

The shift is subtle but profound. She begins saving her inner world for him. When she has a hard day, she messages him first. When she feels misunderstood, she runs to him emotionally. Her husband becomes the provider of logistics, bills, routines, and chores—while the other man becomes the provider of emotional warmth.

This is the core of emotional replacement: the moment she stops reaching for her partner and starts reaching for another man. She does not need sex to feel like she is cheating. She needs an emotional sanctuary—and she has found it elsewhere.

Women who emotionally cheat often do so because they are starving for one of four things:

Validation:

He makes her feel attractive, intelligent, admired, interesting. She feels visible again.

Understanding:

He listens without defensiveness or minimization.
He reflects her feelings back to her.

Comfort:

He soothes her anxieties, praises her efforts, supports her dreams.

Romantic attention:

He calls her beautiful, compliments her presence, notices her vulnerabilities.

Emotional replacement is dangerous because it feels righteous.

She tells herself she deserves to be understood. She deserves to be seen. She deserves compassion. She believes she is simply meeting unmet needs—not betraying her husband.

But every emotional confession is a brick removed from her marriage and laid at the feet of another man. She will start comparing them:

> He listens; her husband interrupts.
> He encourages; her husband criticizes.
> He is warm; her husband has grown cold.

The comparison becomes the fuel that drives the new attachment. Soon, she fantasizes about what life would be like with him. He becomes her escape. He becomes her secret safe place. He becomes the man she thinks of when she cannot sleep.

Women rarely wake up and decide to cheat physically. They drift. They emotionally migrate. They build emotional loyalty outside the marriage until the husband becomes emotionally obsolete.

When emotional replacement is complete, the sexual act is simply a formality—the body confirming what the heart already abandoned.

This is why emotional cheating wounds men so deeply. A physical affair is an action. An emotional replacement is a declaration: "Someone else has your role." Not because she wanted sex with him, but because she wanted *connection* from him.

Chapter 21

Fantasy Relationship: Imagining a Life With Someone Else, Romantic Daydreaming

When a woman begins cheating, the first betrayal is often internal. Before she texts another man, before she meets him, before she touches anyone else, she begins to *live in her head* with someone who is not her husband. Fantasy is the earliest stage of emotional infidelity, subtle, silent, and incredibly powerful.

This is not a random celebrity crush or innocent admiration. It is a *private alternate universe* where another man becomes the solution to everything she feels is missing at home. She imagines what life would be like if he were her partner, how he would treat her, talk to her, protect her, and celebrate her. In her mind, he becomes the man her husband "should have been."

How it begins

Fantasy relationships typically start in moments of emotional pain:

> feeling unseen, unheard, unappreciated,
> longing for affection or attention,
> feeling neglected sexually or emotionally,
> exhaustion from routine, motherhood, or stress.

She starts imagining:

> conversations that never happened
> scenarios where he rescues or cherishes her
> vacations, intimacy, or even a future marriage with him.

This becomes addictive because fantasy has no responsibility, no conflict, no disappointment. Reality has bills, fatigue, arguments, children, chores, aging. Fantasy has none of that. It is pure attention and romance, untouched by accountability.

"He would treat me better."

The most dangerous part is *comparison*.

The fantasy version of the other man is always patient. Always attentive. Always excited to see her. He never dismisses her feelings, never forgets her birthday, never raises his voice.

She does not imagine him angry, stressed, insecure, distracted, or flawed. She imagines him perfect, because her mind edits out anything that doesn't fit the dream.

Meanwhile, her husband becomes the villain in her psychological story:

> the one who doesn't understand her
> the one who is too busy
> the one who has changed
> the one who doesn't "see her".

The fantasy man becomes the emotional hero.

Fantasy is the emotional version of pornography

Just as porn presents unrealistic sexual expectations, romantic fantasy presents *unrealistic emotional expectations.* He is not a real partner. He is a highlight reel, a projection of her unmet needs: attention, affection, admiration, romance, excitement, novelty.

She escapes into thoughts of him during chores, work, loneliness, or conflict. He becomes her mental refuge.

When imagination becomes betrayal

Fantasy becomes cheating the moment *she chooses it over connection.* She begins to protect the fantasy.

> She hides her thoughts from her husband.
> She thinks about the other man before bed.
> She imagines conversations instead of having real ones.
> She romanticizes even tiny interactions. ("He smiled at me, maybe he's the one")

Fantasy also influences her behavior: she becomes colder at home, less motivated sexually, emotionally distant, dismissive, resentful, and harder to please. She stops trying to repair the relationship because mentally, she has already replaced it.

The husband feels something has changed, but cannot name it. He only senses the distance.

The cruel truth

Fantasy cheating is often worse than physical cheating because it rewrites reality itself. A man can forgive a mistake. But how do you compete with a perfect version of another man who exists only in her imagination? In fantasy, he always says the right thing. He always touches her gently. He always knows what she needs. He never makes mistakes.

No real husband can compete with that.

The emotional migration

Fantasy is not innocent. It is a migration of loyalty. First, she gives him her thoughts. Then she gives him her hopes. Then she gives him her dreams.

And one day, she might give him her body.

Women rarely cheat first with their hands. They cheat with their *hearts and imaginations*. By the time a woman has built a romantic world around another man in her mind, she has already left the relationship in the place that matters most: her emotional future.

Affair of the Heart With a Coworker: Sharing Details She Denies Her Husband

An emotional affair with a coworker does not start in the bedroom — it starts in the breakroom. It begins with subtle exchanges: a lingering smile, a shared joke after a meeting, a sympathetic "Rough day?" when she looks tired. Someone who sees her without the history, pressure, or expectations of home.

Coworkers share something powerful: proximity. They experience the same stress, projects, deadlines, victories, frustrations, and ambitions. They see each other at their best, dressed well, competent, collected, not exhausted in sweatpants after a long day of parenting or arguments. The office becomes fertile ground for emotional intimacy.

How it begins

She opens up. At first, it's about work: annoying clients, an overwhelmed boss, stressful deadlines. Then it shifts:

"I'm tired of being the only one who tries at home."
"He never listens."
"I feel invisible."

She tells him things she does *not* tell her husband. She fills him with the private emotional currency of her marriage.

Her coworker is not carrying the weight of her real life. He is not the father of her children, not the one juggling bills, not the one managing chores, not the one who sees her unfiltered.

He sees the *edited version* of her: the professional, the competent, the attractive, the interesting. And she sees the edited version of him.

Why it feels safe

A workplace affair begins with *justification*:

"We're just friends."
"Everyone vents."
"He understands me."
"He's harmless."

The husband, meanwhile, becomes emotionally starved. He gets the silence, the cold shoulders, the "I'm fine." Her coworker gets the vulnerability, the laughter, the gratitude, the *heart*.

This is where the betrayal begins: not when she kisses him, but when she gives him the emotional access her husband used to receive.

Why the coworker becomes irresistible

He doesn't see the side of her that is angry, exhausted, overwhelmed. He sees competence, independence, and intelligence. He compliments her work, her ideas, her creativity. He admires her ambition in ways her husband may not understand. She feels validated, not as a wife or mother, but as *a woman*.

She tells herself: "He sees the real me." But the truth is darker: He sees the *version of her that costs nothing*.

She begins to fantasize:

"If I were with him, I'd be happier."
"He would support my goals."
"He would listen."
"He would treat me better."

These thoughts are not harmless. They are *infidelity in seed form*.

What she gives him that she withholds from her husband

She shares:

her frustrations,
her insecurities,
her dreams,
her ambitions,
her unfiltered emotions,
her emotional hunger.

She withholds:

Patience,
softness,
romantic curiosity,
gratitude,
sexual energy,
vulnerability.

Her husband gets the residue; her coworker gets the radiance.

The emotional spiral

Soon, she becomes dependent:

> She checks her phone during meetings.
> She waits for his reply.
> She tells herself she doesn't need her husband's affection anymore.
> She starts blaming the marriage for everything she now feels deprived of.

The fantasy becomes more vibrant than the relationship she actually lives in. The coworker becomes the *emotional safe haven*; the husband becomes the *emotional landfill*. And here is the painful paradox: *the coworker is not better; he is simply untested.*

He has not seen her sick. He has not seen her depressed. He has not seen her angry in the middle of a real argument. He has not carried the emotional weight of loving her through years of hardship. He sees her curated life; her husband sees her whole life. That is why emotional affairs at work are so seductive: they operate on highlight reels, not reality.

When the betrayal becomes undeniable

The moment she:

> deletes messages,
> edits conversations,
> hides notifications,
> stays late "to finish a project,"
> dresses up for office events with him in mind,
> tells her husband, "You're overreacting", or
> gets defensive at the mention of the coworker,

the affair has already happened—not physically, but emotionally.

Because an affair of the heart is not measured by sex; It is measured by *loyalty*.

Once her feelings migrate to another man, her husband hasn't just lost her body; he has lost the center of her emotional life, and she gave it away one conversation at a time.

Reconnecting With an Old Flame: Nostalgia, Messages, "I Wonder What Could've Been."

Nothing tempts the human heart like memory. When a woman reconnects with someone she once loved, she is not just speaking to a person. She is speaking to a past version of herself. She is talking to whom she *was* before responsibility, before children, before exhaustion, before disappointment. And that can be intoxicating.

Old flames carry a unique psychological power:

> They require no introduction, no effort, no discovery.
> He already knows her history, her childhood, the way she laughed in her twenties, the dreams she once had.
> He remembers her when she felt alive, hopeful, exciting, when she believed she could be anything.

So when modern stress crushes her, when her marriage becomes dull or suffocating, a message from him becomes a portal.

It starts quietly:

> "Hey stranger."
> "I just found an old picture of us."
> "Remember that night…?"

And suddenly she is no longer a wife in a routine marriage; she is the girl who once felt desired, special, fearless.

Nostalgia is the seducer

She is not necessarily in love with him. She is in love with the *version of herself he unlocks*: the youthful self, the adventurous self, the carefree self. The brain rewrites memory, polishing the past and deleting the pain. The arguments, the incompatibilities, the breakups, the tears—all fade. What remains is *the highlight reel of young love*.

She tells herself she is "just catching up," but the emotional shift is already happening:

> She checks his social media more than she should.
> She reads old messages.
> She thinks about him before going to bed.
> She wonders what life would look like if they had stayed together.

It doesn't matter whether the old flame lives in another city, has his own family, or is married; nostalgia makes him feel like destiny.

The slippery slope

> Reconnection becomes intimacy.
> Intimacy becomes exclusivity.
> Exclusivity becomes secrecy.

She begins sharing details she never planned to reveal:

"My husband doesn't listen anymore."
"I feel alone most days."
"Sometimes I regret the choices I've made."

He replies with the exact words she wants to hear:

"You deserved better."
"If I had known, I never would've let you go."
"We had something special."

This is how emotional affairs accelerate. Not through novelty, but through *familiarity*.

Why husbands lose this battle before it begins

The old flame does not see her bills, her insecurities, her post-partum body, her stress, her flaws. He sees the *idealized memory* she carries in her mind. He never had to live with her daily reality. He never saw her angry, exhausted, resentful, overwhelmed, or fragile. To him, she is forever frozen in the golden age of youth.

And she reciprocates. She does not see him as he truly is now; she sees the boy who kissed her in the car, who held her in the dark, who promised he would never leave. He is not a man. He is a *time machine*.

The quiet betrayal

Reconnecting with an old flame is rarely loud at first: no screaming, no hotel rooms, no dramatic exits. It begins with whispers:

"It's crazy how much I've thought of you."
"I still remember that summer."
"I never felt that way again."

Those words feel safe. They feel sentimental. They feel personal and special.

But nostalgia is not harmless. It is emotional infidelity wearing the perfume of the past.

The mental migration

When she starts comparing the *remembered* version of him to the *imperfect* version of her husband, the relationship is already collapsing. Her husband is measured against a ghost, a memory cleaned of flaws, a man who exists only in hindsight.

He cannot compete with that. No husband can. Because the old flame is not a person; he is a *shortcut to romantic fantasy* and the woman she *wishes* she still was.

And in those quiet messages, filled with nostalgia and "What if...," she has already cheated, long before she ever touches another body.

Chapter 24

Validation From Compliments: Living on Attention From Male Friends or Strangers

A woman does not need to fall in love to cheat. Sometimes, all it takes is attention. When she begins to feed on validation from other men, she is not simply being "social." She is outsourcing her self-worth.

How it starts

It often begins quietly, especially when she feels:

> unappreciated at home
> overlooked by her husband
> taken for granted
> constantly criticized
> invisible as a woman, only seen as a mother, wife, helper.

So when a man says, "You look beautiful today," it hits like a drug. Not because of him, but because of what she has been starving for.

Compliments become oxygen:

> a cashier who calls her "miss",
> a coworker who notices her perfume,
> a gym trainer who says "You're strong,"
> a guy on Instagram who replies to her selfie,
> an old friend who messages after years of silence.

Each comment becomes a micro-dose of validation. And soon she begins to crave it.

Attention becomes a hobby

She dresses a little nicer when she knows he will be there. She angles her photos to get more likes. She posts thirst traps disguised as "fitness progress" or "outfit of the day." She watches the notifications like a gambler watches slot machines.

Every ping, every emoji, every DM says: "You are still desirable."

Her husband may have said it for years, but marriage has normalized it. Validation from outsiders isn't just praise; it is *proof.* Proof that she can still attract. Proof that someone still sees her. Proof that she is more than laundry, kids, errands, and routine.

The emotional corruption

Attention becomes addictive because it is effortless: no intimacy required, no accountability, no vulnerability. Only approval. She doesn't have to be kind, patient, or loving. She doesn't need to give anything in return except access to her skin, her smile, or her time.

Compliments from strangers feel cleaner than affection from her husband, because:

Strangers don't know her flaws.
They aren't tired of her patterns.
They don't argue with her.
They see only her highlight reel.

She becomes the curator of her own desirability.

She creates situations to receive praise

She finds opportunities to be complimented:

"Does this look okay?"
posts gym selfies,
"I feel so ugly today", baiting reassurance,
flirtatious stories,
provocative clothing at social events,
intentionally long eye contact,
letting men "accidentally" flirt.

All of this is masked as self-expression or self-care, but secretly it is *validation hunting*.

And every time a man gives her what she wants, her emotional loyalty shifts a little further away from her husband.

The invisible betrayal

The pain for the partner lies not in what she does openly, but in what she *needs* privately. She no longer seeks her husband's admiration; she seeks admiration *instead of him*. His compliments feel familiar; theirs feel electrifying. What used to make her blush at home now barely moves her, because she has learned to measure her worth in *strangers' reactions*, not her partner's devotion.

The shift is subtle but lethal

Soon,

> She stops caring how her husband sees her,
> She cares more about how male followers see her,
> She downplays his affection,
> She magnifies theirs,
> She dismisses his compliments,
> She screenshots theirs,
> She ignores his needs,
> She feeds on their attention.

She may never send a nude or kiss another man. But she has already *left the marriage emotionally*, draining intimacy from her husband and feeding it to unknown men.

Why this hurts men deeply

Men do not just fear losing their wife to another man. They fear losing her to a crowd. Not a single rival, but a thousand faceless admirers who don't have to work or sacrifice.

He gave her loyalty, stability, sacrifice, and commitment. They give her emojis, likes, "You're gorgeous." And in her mind, those things begin to feel equal, even superior.

Venting to Another Man About Her Marriage: Emotional Betrayal Disguised as Friendship

A woman does not have to take off her clothes to cheat. All she has to do is take her *pain*, the part of her she once gave to her husband, and hand it to another man. That is where the emotional affair begins: not with sex, not with flirting, but with *confession*.

The gateway: "He's just someone I talk to."

It starts softly. A coworker, an online acquaintance, a gym buddy, an old friend, a man she barely knows. He asks a simple question: "Are you okay?" And she answers him in ways she has stopped answering her husband.

She chooses him because

> he listens without interrupting,
> he doesn't challenge her,

he isn't emotionally invested in the conflict.
he never tells her she is wrong.

What begins as casual comfort quickly becomes emotional outsourcing.

How it unfolds

She complains about small things at first: "I'm exhausted," "He doesn't help with anything," "We're not communicating."

He responds: "That sounds hard," "You deserve better," "I'd never treat someone like that."

In those moments, she experiences something addictive: *validation without accountability.*

Her husband has a history with her. He has seen her flaws, her bad moods, her patterns, her mistakes. He pushes back, argues, challenges her. He is invested in the truth. The other man has no such burden. He has no stake in honesty. He has every incentive to play the savior.

Emotional cheating masquerading as support

The dynamic deepens. She goes to him first when she is angry. She goes to him again when she is sad. She goes to him when she is lonely. She goes to him when she needs understanding.

Part of her brain begins recording:

> *He listens.*
> *He cares.*
> *He gets it.*
> *He gets me.*

And every new venting session becomes a thread binding them together. Her husband becomes the cause of pain; the other man becomes the cure.

Why this form of cheating is so dangerous

Because it feels *morally clean*.
There is no hotel room.
No secret kiss.
No naked pictures.

She convinces herself:

"We're just friends."
"He's a good listener."
"I need someone to talk to."
"My husband isn't emotionally available."

But hidden beneath these excuses is the truth: she is releasing intimacy to a man who has not earned it. Every emotional secret she shares whittles away at the marriage.

The psychological shift

Venting to another man does two devastating things:

1. It rewrites the story of her marriage.

She talks about her husband's flaws.
The other man sees only the worst version of him.
She never talks about his strengths, commitment, or sacrifices.
She paints herself as the wounded heroine, and him as the villain.

2. It idealizes the other man.

He only hears her pain, not her imperfections.
He comforts, so he seems compassionate.

He sympathizes, so he seems loyal.

He validates, so he seems emotionally superior.

She forgets that he is reacting to a curated narrative. *This is where betrayal becomes undeniable.* The moment she thinks, *I can't tell my husband this… but I can tell him.*

That is the boundary crossed.

She hides messages.

She deletes call logs.

She changes his contact name.

She explains her mood with vague excuses.

She becomes defensive when his name is mentioned.

She is no longer venting. She is choosing another man *over the one she vowed to stand beside.*

Why men see this as worse than physical cheating

Because emotional cheating is not about sex, it is about *loyalty.* A man can forgive a drunken mistake. But how does he compete with the man who knows her fears, the man who knows her childhood, the man who knows every detail of their marriage, the man who is allowed into her most vulnerable places?

The other man becomes the emotional version of a lover. He has access to her heart. He has access to her wounds. He has access to the part of her that marriage was supposed to protect.

The painful truth

Women call it "just talking." Men call it what it is: *You're giving another man the part of yourself you should be giving to me.* And once she hands her pain, her secrets, and her emotional trust to someone else, the marriage has already been violated, long before her body ever leaves the room.

Chapter 26

The "Work Husband" or Gym Partner: Comfort, Partnership, Inside Jokes, and the Disappearance of Boundaries

One of the most socially acceptable forms of infidelity is the "work husband" or the "gym partner." It looks harmless from the outside. It looks like companionship, support, a buddy. But emotionally, it is often *a replacement husband wearing a friendly label.*

Women don't usually fall into these arrangements by accident. They *slide* into them—quietly, gradually, with interactions that feel innocent at first:

> sharing snacks or lunches,
> texting about schedules or meetings,
> taking breaks together,
> trading jokes,

complaining about stress,
staying late "just to finish this one thing."

The husband at home gets the leftovers of her energy; the man at work or the gym gets her *best version*: the polished, smiling, social version of her.

The psychological trap

Unlike an affair of passion, the "work husband" is built on daily contact and shared struggle: they joke about their boss, they motivate each other during workouts, they celebrate small wins, they cheer each other up on bad days.

He becomes her emotional teammate. He sees her effort. He praises her discipline. He tells her she is doing a great job. He compliments her outfits when her real husband barely notices she changed her hair.

This dynamic creates a powerful illusion: "He understands me better than my actual husband."

The intimacy hides in the routine

The moments are small but constant:

a hand on her shoulder when she's stressed,
a "You got this" before a presentation,
a wink after a shared joke,
a DM that says, "You're killing it today,"
a text at night about something that "reminded him of her."

They never discuss love. They never say, "We're cheating." But they are sharing *emotional territory* that belongs to her marriage.

The boundary breakdown

It starts with humor, inside jokes no one else gets, memes they send only to each other, nicknames. The husband at home becomes "the serious one"; the gym partner becomes "the fun one." He knows her favorite protein shake flavor. He knows she hates leg day. He knows when she's ovulating because she complains about cramps.

These are *husband-level details*, but they're falling into the hands of another man.

Why this form of cheating is so easily denied

Because there is no sex. No kissing. No confession. So she tells herself:

> *We're just close.*
> *He's like a brother.*
> *I need support at work.*
> *He motivates me.*

But emotional loyalty is already migrating. Even if nothing physical happens, she has created an exclusive emotional lane, a private road that her husband cannot access. The other man becomes *her emotional comfort*; her husband becomes *her responsibility*.

The gym partner variant

The gym is one of the most potent breeding grounds for emotional affairs:

> physical vulnerability,
> shared exhaustion,
> compliments on appearance,
> body contact during spotting,
> hormone surges,
> sweat, adrenaline, victory.

Cheating doesn't start with sex. It starts when he says: "Wow, you're getting so strong." or "He must be crazy not to appreciate you." She feels desired, admired, visible. And it's even more seductive when she earns it through effort: he watches her work, sweat, progress, improve.

That creates intimacy without words.

The husband senses it

He asks:

> "Why do you talk about him so much?"
> "You're texting him again?"
> "Why does he need you after hours?"
> "Why does he know things I don't?"

She reacts:

> "You're jealous."
> "You're insecure."
> "You're paranoid."

But she knows the truth: If she has to hide how much they joke, text, or talk, it has already crossed the line.

The brutal reality

A "work husband" or gym partner is not a friend. It is a *parallel relationship*. It is someone who:

> gets her laughter,
> gets her gratitude,
> gets her praise,
> gets her emotional honesty,
> gets her best energy.

Her real husband gets:

> Complaints,

silence,
exhaustion,
frustration.

And eventually, he gets a version of her who has already given her intimacy to someone else.

Why this wounds men deeply

Men don't fear the one-night stand. They fear the man she trusts. They fear the man she smiles for. The man she texts on her lunch break. The man who sees her shine when she no longer shines at home. Because that man is not "just a friend." He is the recipient of the emotional loyalty she withdrew from the marriage.

A "work husband" is not a joke. It is a slow-motion affair of the heart, and hearts cheat long before bodies ever do.

Chapter 27

Posting Seductive Photos: Not for Her Husband, but for Other Men

A woman doesn't need to cheat physically to abandon her partner. Sometimes, all she has to do is put herself on display, not for love, not for confidence, but for attention from men who are not her husband.

It begins with a simple realization: her husband's validation no longer excites her. But strangers' attention does.

So she posts a photo. Not a family picture. Not a casual selfie. Not a memory. A carefully crafted image:

> low-cut angles,
> gym leggings,
> bikini shots,
> thirst-trap mirror selfies,
> suggestive poses,

"accidental" cleavage,

lips slightly parted,

captions that appear innocent but invite compliments.

She says it's "just empowerment," but the truth is deeper: she is fishing for attention.

She wants men to look, not him

If the goal were to attract her husband, she would send him the photo privately. She would text, "Do you like this?" She would ask him to admire her. But instead she posts it publicly:

Instagram

TikTok

Snap

Facebook stories

Private groups

Close friends lists

Secret accounts ("Finstas")

She is not inviting love; she is inviting *desire*.

The dopamine economy

Social media taps into primal psychology:

likes = approval

comments = validation

DMs = desire

shares = popularity

thirsty messages = power

And once she tastes it, she wants more. That small dopamine hit after 10 likes becomes the craving for 100. One thirsty comment becomes ten. One explicit message becomes dozens. She tells herself:

I'm confident.
It's my body.
I should be allowed to express myself.
You're insecure if it bothers you.

But what she really means is: "I no longer seek validation from you; I get it from them."

Why this is emotional infidelity

Because it is rooted in the rejection of the husband as the primary audience. She doesn't just display her body; she weaponizes it. Not to seduce her partner, but to provoke desire in strangers. She creates a marketplace for her sexuality, and then says, "I owe you nothing for it."

Meanwhile, her husband watches her

> bending for the camera,
> exaggerating curves,
> adjusting lighting,
> taking 20 shots to find the perfect pose,
> smoothing skin with filters, and
> arching her back for strangers.

He sees her invest more time in online seduction than in intimacy at home.

The hidden betrayal: private attention

The real infidelity doesn't happen in the comments. It happens in the DMs:

> "You're gorgeous."
> "You're so sexy."
> "Why is your husband so lucky?"
> "You should model."
> "If you were mine…"

She responds with:

> Emojis,
> thanks,
> "haha stoppp,"
> hearts,
> playful denial.

Every reply is a quiet invitation: "Keep feeding me."

She may not meet these men in person, but she has already crossed a boundary: she has stopped showing up for her husband and started showing up for an audience.

The moral inversion

Her husband becomes the *critic*:

> "Do you really need to post that?"
> "Who was that guy commenting?"
> "Why are you dressed like that online?"

She reacts:

> "You're controlling."
> "You're insecure."
> "It's my body."
> "You don't trust me."

She paints him as the oppressor and herself as the victim of policing. In reality, she has reversed the roles: she betrays him publicly, then blames him for noticing.

Why men feel this betrayal deeply

Because it is a humiliation.

He watches other men:

lust after his wife,
joke about her body,
save her pictures,
screenshot her photos. and
DM her behind his back.

He does not feel like a partner. He feels like a cuckolded spectator. And she knows it. That is why she posts anyway. Because somewhere inside her, she no longer wants *his* desire. She wants everyone else's.

Posting seductive photos is not harmless self-expression. It is the digital version of walking naked into a room of men and pretending the husband should not care. It is not about empowerment. It is about replacing the intimacy of marriage with the attention of strangers.

Chapter 28

Online Emotional Bonds: DMs, Comments, and Long Digital Relationships

Online cheating is not defined by nudity, sex, or physical meetings. It is defined by *emotional displacement*: giving her attention, vulnerability, and affection to a man she has never met, sometimes for months or years. Online emotional bonds are especially dangerous because they feel *safe*. They happen behind screens, inside apps, under usernames, and in spaces her husband never checks.

It starts with small interactions:

A like.
A heart emoji.
A comment on a selfie.
A compliment from a stranger.

Then comes the first message: "Haha thank you!" or "I appreciate that :)"

That message is the spark. Slowly, the digital stranger becomes a digital confidant. They start talking about:

> gym progress,
> career stress,
> insecurities,
> dreams,
> her husband's flaws,
> how misunderstood she feels.

He responds with empathy and admiration:

> "You deserve someone who gets you."
> "I don't know how he could ever ignore you."
> "You're amazing. I'd never treat you that way."

This is how online affairs grow—not through sex apps, but through *validation ecosystems.*

The algorithm becomes her emotional environment

Social media rewards her:

> She posts → he likes it.
> She complains → he comforts her.
> She hints at pain → he always replies.

She begins to anticipate his presence: she checks whether he viewed her story, she refreshes her notifications, she replies to him first, she reads his messages before her husband's. He becomes the invisible partner.

What makes online emotional cheating so seductive?

Because it is incomplete. Incomplete relationships are intoxicating. He never sees her flaws:

> the messy hair,
> the postpartum body,
> the stress, anger, depression,
> her worst moods,
> her insecurities when she wakes up.

He only sees *curated pieces of her life*: edited, filtered, tailored for attention.

And she only sees the best parts of him. He becomes

> charming,
> attentive,
> emotionally available,
> flattering,
> consistent, and
> always online.

Meanwhile, her husband

> works,
> sleeps,
> is tired,
> is stressed,
> forgets anniversaries, and
> speaks bluntly.

Online men don't share bills or chores; they only share emotions and fantasy.

She tells herself it's harmless

She rationalizes:

> "We're just talking."
> "He's just a friend."
> "It's just online."
> "You're overreacting."

But then:

> She hides messages.
> She deletes chats.
> She archives conversations.
> She changes his name in her phone.
> She blocks him from her husband's account. No one hides what is innocent.

The slow replacement

Without noticing it, she begins to *emotionally migrate*:

> She messages him when she wakes up.
> She scrolls through his page during lunch.
> She chats with him in the bathroom at night.
> She runs to him when her husband upsets her.

Her husband feels a distance he cannot name. She is in the same bed, but her attention belongs to someone in another city, another state, another country.

Why this form of cheating is so toxic

Because it builds in silence. No physical encounter. No lipstick on the collar. No suspicious receipts. Only hours—hours stolen from her husband and invested in a stranger.

Online emotional affairs last longer than physical ones because they exist without risk:

> no pregnancy,
> no STD,
> no hotel bills,
> no witnesses,
> no guilt triggered by physical touch.

It's all dopamine and imagination.

And then comes the escalation. One day she sends a selfie. He compliments it. She sends a slightly more revealing one. He reacts strongly. She sends a video. He asks for more. He confesses feelings. Fantasy becomes desire, desire becomes loyalty, loyalty becomes betrayal.

Even if they never meet, she has already left her marriage emotionally.

Online emotional cheating is not a glitch of technology. It is *emotional infidelity with no friction*: easy to start, effortless to escalate, and nearly impossible for a spouse to detect... until the damage is already done.

Secret Friendships: Hiding Them Because She Knows Her Husband Wouldn't Approve

A woman does not need sex to betray her marriage. Sometimes, all she needs is a friendship she intentionally **keeps in the dark.** The secrecy itself is the confession. It starts with "He's just a friend."

Not a boyfriend. Not a lover. Just someone she talks to "here and there." But friendships are not defined by labels; they are defined by *access*. She gives this man access to

> her thoughts,
> her moods,
> her struggles,
> her personal life,
> her vulnerabilities. and
> her ambitions.

And she denies that access to her husband. That is the moment the bond becomes dangerous.

The friendship has rules she does not tell her husband about: the messages, the calls, the late-night conversations, the inside jokes, the emotional moments. She starts deleting texts. She turns off notifications. She messages him when the husband is asleep. She acts differently when the husband walks into the room.

Healthy friendships do not require hiding. Affairs do.

Why secrecy matters

If something is innocent, it survives in daylight. If it needs to be hidden, it is already infidelity. She might tell herself:

> *I don't want drama.*
> *He wouldn't understand*
> *It's none of his business.*
> *We're just talking.*

But the real reason is buried in emotion: *she knows she is giving another man a piece of herself she should be giving to her husband.*

Emotional safe zones

The secret friend becomes her comfort, her validation, her escape, a place to be admired, a place to be interesting again, someone who listens without reminding her of responsibilities. She messages him when she feels misunderstood. She confides in him when her marriage feels strained. She runs to him emotionally when her husband disappoints her.

He becomes Plan A for emotional intimacy; her husband becomes Plan B.

The mental divide

She begins to divide her life into two parts:

The public relationship — what she shows her husband.

The private relationship — what she shares with the other man.

Every secret message is a small betrayal. Every deleted chat is a decision. Every excuse is an admission. It is not the content of the conversation that matters; it is the direction of the intimacy.

Why this wounds men deeply

Men don't fear strangers flirting with their wives. They fear the man who knows

> her stress,
> her insecurities,
> her childhood,
> her arguments,
> her fears,
> her dreams, and
> her emotional triggers.

Because that man has something more intimate than her body: *her trust.* She may not sleep with him… yet. But emotional cheating always moves on a timeline:

1. Innocent Conversation
2. Regular Chatting
3. Private Jokes
4. Vulnerability
5. Loyalty
6. Fantasy
7. Boundary Crossing
8. Physical Contact

She will insist she "never planned anything." Yet she is already building a bridge from curiosity to desire.

The moment that reveals everything

If she is forced to choose: show her husband the messages, or stop talking to the "friend", she will choose the man she is loyal to. And very often, *that is not her husband.*

Secret friendships are not friendships at all. They are affairs in incubation, born from the simple truth: if she has to hide it, she has already betrayed him.

Chapter 30

Physical Affair: Sexual Encounters With Someone Else

A physical affair is the most visible form of infidelity, but it is rarely the beginning. Sex is usually the final expression of a long emotional migration. It is the moment she crosses the boundary she once swore she never would. Not because she suddenly became reckless, but because the marriage has already been replaced internally.

It rarely starts with sex

Most physical affairs begin in places that look harmless:

> a gym partner she laughs with,
> a coworker who "gets her,"
> an old flame she reconnects with,
> an online stranger she flirts with,
> someone who compliments her appearance,
> the person she vents to about her husband.

For weeks or months, the lines blur:

> flirtation,
> private texting,
> emotional vulnerability,
> shared excitement,
> secret meetings,
> excuses…

a kiss that she doesn't stop.
After that, the slope is no longer slippery; it becomes a slide.

The first time is not an accident

She will tell herself:

> "It just happened."
> "I got carried away."
> "I was vulnerable."
> "It was the alcohol."
> "He made me feel alive."

But the truth is simpler: *affairs are prepared, not spontaneous.*
She knew when she

> shaved differently,
> wore perfume she never wears at home,
> chose lingerie under her outfit,
> positioned her hair,
> selected the dress that turns heads,
> did her makeup with intention.

She did not dress for her husband; she dressed for the man she was going to betray him with.

Why physical betrayal hurts differently

Sex is not just a biological act. It is a declaration of preference. For a husband, the pain comes from the body saying: "You are no longer the one I choose." He imagines things he cannot unsee:

> another man's hands on her,
> her breathing differently,
> the sounds she makes,
> her body opening to someone else,
> the intimacy he believed was exclusive to him.

It is not just the sex. It is the *sanctity* of it. Sex in marriage is not a hobby. It is the language of trust. To give it away is to tear the foundation from under the relationship.

The "dual life"

She begins to live in two worlds.

With her husband:

> Dinner,
> chores,
> routine,
> obligation,
> numbness.

With her lover:

> Excitement,
> youth,
> adrenaline,
> praise,
> fantasy.

She becomes addicted to contrast: The thrill of being desired by someone new versus the comfort of being known by someone old. She will justify every step:

> *I deserve happiness.*
> *He pushed me away.*
> *I was lonely.*
> *He ignored me.*
> *We were dead anyway.*

Cheating feels like rebirth. Until the cost arrives.

The aftermath: the body tells the truth

She becomes distant. Her touch changes. Her eyes avoid his. Her hugs are shorter. Her sex is mechanical or disappears entirely.

She may shower longer. Do laundry separately. Keep her phone glued to her hand. Check her reflection before errands. Come home late and offer vague answers.

A woman's body cannot hide its betrayal: *it stops belonging to the person she betrayed.*

The most dangerous part

A physical affair does not simply replace a sexual partner. It replaces an identity. Men feel it even if they don't know the details:

> They feel replaced as a lover.
> They feel rejected as a man.
> They feel humiliated as a husband.
> They feel erased as a protector.

Cheating isn't just sleeping with another man; it is sleeping with another future. A one-time mistake can be confessed. A sustained physical affair becomes a second relationship.

A physical affair is not a single act of adultery. It is the moment a woman chooses another man's hands, eyes, breath, pleasure, *and in doing so, she kills the marriage in the most primal way possible.*

Chapter 31

Revenge Sex: Cheating Because She Felt Betrayed, Neglected, or Hurt

Revenge sex is not about lust. It is about punishment, power, and emotional warfare. It happens when a woman feels wounded, not just by infidelity, but by neglect, rejection, emotional abandonment, disrespect, or humiliation. She does not cheat because she is attracted. She cheats because she wants her partner to feel what she felt.

Revenge sex is a statement: "You hurt me, so I will hurt you back."

It begins with a wound

Sometimes it is obvious:

> He cheated.
> He flirted openly.
> He lied.
> He dismissed her pain.
> He ignored her needs.

Sometimes it's quieter:

> He stopped touching her.
> He made her feel invisible.
> He never complimented her.
> He chose work or hobbies over her.
> He mocked her insecurities.
> He compared her to other women.

She internalizes a message: "I am not valued by the man I love."

When pain becomes a weapon

The moment she chooses another man, the goal becomes emotional retaliation:

> "I want him to know what it feels like."
> "I want him to lose sleep."
> "I want him to feel jealousy."
> "I want him to see I can be wanted."
> "I want him to regret hurting me."

This is not cheating *to feel good*. It is cheating *to make him feel bad*.

Why revenge sex is more brutal than a normal affair

Because it is *intentional*. She does not slip. She does not fall into temptation. She makes a decision: "If you can betray me, then I can betray you too." In her mind, the act becomes *justice*. Even if the relationship was already dying, even if intimacy was already gone, *revenge cheating is never about healing, only destruction.*

The psychology behind it

Revenge sex is fueled by:

Rage,
humiliation,
insecurity,
competition,
resentment,
abandonment,
a need to reclaim power.

It is a temporary anesthetic: "If I hurt him, maybe the pain in my chest will stop."

But the aftermath is far worse:

The guilt returns.
The shame grows.
The trust becomes unrecoverable.
She learns she is capable of violence.

Because revenge sex is not emotional; it is *ego-driven cruelty disguised as empowerment.*

The "target"

The man she chooses for revenge is rarely random. It may be:

someone who has shown interest before,
an ex who still wants her,
a coworker who flirts,
a trainer who compliments her,
a friend she knows is attracted to her,
a stranger who gives her validation.

But the key is always the same: He is accessible, and he is willing. She does not need love. She needs an audience.

The aftermath: self-sabotage masquerading as victory

After the act, she will tell herself:

> *Now we're even.*
> *He deserved it.*
> *I proved my worth.*
> *He shouldn't have hurt me.*

But revenge is corrosive. She learns something ugly: *she can betray too.* That knowledge does not empower her. It destabilizes her identity:

> She feels disgust in the mirror,
> She panics at the thought of confessing,
> She becomes paranoid that he will find out,
> She starts comparing the two men,
> She rewrites history to justify herself.

She may even escalate to avoid guilt: she cheats again, so the first one doesn't feel like a mistake.

Why revenge sex destroys a marriage instantly

Because it does not say: "I found comfort elsewhere." It says: "I chose to hurt you."

A husband can sometimes forgive cheating caused by fear, loneliness, or emotional confusion. He cannot forgive cheating done specifically to wound him. To him, the message is:

> "You are replaceable."
> "Your pain is my satisfaction."
> "I want to humiliate you."

Revenge sex does not just break trust. *It kills the possibility of repair.*

Chapter 32

Sexual Texting and Photos: Sending Nudes, Sexting, and Explicit Messages

Sexual texting is cheating long before any physical encounter occurs. Because when a woman sends her body through a screen, she is giving someone else the sexual access meant for her partner. It is not "just pictures" or "just words." It is intimacy transferred, desire redirected, and loyalty broken.

The psychological seduction

Most sexting begins with playful curiosity:

> flirty emojis,
> compliments,
> "innocent" selfies,
> jokes with double meanings,
> late-night messages.

Then it escalates:

> "Show me more."
> "You look amazing."
> "I bet you're even better without that outfit."
> "If you were here right now…"

She responds not because it is physical, but because it is *attention*. Her partner at home sees her body as familiar. The man online sees it as treasure. The newness intoxicates her.

Sending nudes is not accidental

A nude photo—the angle, the pose, the lighting, the lingerie—is deliberate. She prepares it. She angles the camera. She edits it. She checks the mirror. She re-takes five, ten, fifteen versions until she finds the one that makes her feel powerful. And she sends it; not to her husband, but to another man.

This is not insecurity; it is sexual outsourcing.

The emotional lie she tells herself

Women often rationalize:

> "It's just fantasy."
> "It's harmless."
> "We're not touching."
> "It's only online."
> "It's not real cheating."

But if it wasn't real cheating, she would not hide it:

> deleting photos,
> clearing chat history,
> turning off notifications,

> making private folders,
> using apps that auto-delete messages,
> renaming the contact,
> locking her phone in the bathroom.

No one hides innocence.

Why sexting wounds deeper than physical cheating

A man can forgive his partner kissing someone once. He cannot forgive her posing for another man—adjusting her breasts, arching her back, opening her body—with intention, lighting, and desire. Because sex is an act of the body, but sexting is *an act of the mind and imagination*. A physical affair lasts minutes. A sexting affair lasts hours:

> Typing,
> teasing,
> sending,
> responding,
> anticipating,
> fantasizing.

It becomes a ritual.

The addictive cycle

Sexting is dopamine warfare:

1. She sends a provocative selfie.
2. He reacts with lust, shock, admiration.
3. She feels desired and powerful.
4. She sends something riskier.

The reward is instant: Attention. Validation. Control. Her husband might say: "You look beautiful." The online man says:

"You make me hard."
"I want you right now."
"I'd worship your body."
"I can't stop thinking about you."

The second voice wins.

It is digital, not innocent

She may never touch him in person, but the private camera becomes a stage. The man she sends photos to zooms in, screenshots, saves, shows friends, replays, masturbates to her image. He owns a version of her that her husband doesn't even see anymore. This is not fantasy. It is a transfer of sexual power.

Sex through screens is still sex

Words can be pornographic: describing positions, talking about orgasms, detailing what they would do, commanding her to pose, asking how she would sound, telling her how he would touch her. Their bodies never meet, but their minds are naked together. Their imaginations are in the same bed. And imagination is the birthplace of infidelity.

The silent betrayal

The husband senses it: sudden phone secrecy, bathroom texting, midnight giggles at the screen, seductive selfies she never sends him, lingerie purchased for "herself" but never worn at home.

He asks: "Who are you texting?"
She replies:

"No one."
"You're paranoid."
"It's just a joke."

"It's a friend."

"You're insecure."

But deep down she knows: she is sharing sexual intimacy with someone who isn't her partner.

Sexual texting isn't harmless digital play. It is the slow leak of loyalty. It is the body offered in pixels, the soul offered through conversation, and the marriage traded for *fantasy with a stranger.*

Chapter 33

Affairs With "Safe" Male Friends: The Guy She Insists Is "Just a Friend"

This is one of the most dangerous forms of cheating because it hides behind innocence and social acceptability. She chooses a man who seems harmless: a coworker, gym buddy, old classmate, neighbor, or single dad from the kids' school. He doesn't appear to threaten the marriage, so she allows emotional closeness to grow without guilt. She shares her frustrations, insecurities, and marriage problems with him, things she no longer shares with her husband. He becomes the one who listens without judgment and reacts with admiration instead of criticism. She starts to look forward to seeing him: lunch breaks, workouts, car rides, workplace errands, "quick coffee catch-ups." The friendship becomes her escape, a place where she feels interesting, attractive, and valued.

At home, her husband becomes associated with responsibility, stress, and routine. The "friend" becomes associated with comfort, praise, and emotional relief. The emotional boundary starts cracking:

> She texts him late at night.
> She deletes conversations "to avoid drama."
> She hides his name in her phone or changes it.
> She adjusts the tone of her voice when her partner walks into the room.
> She gets defensive when her husband questions the friendship.

If the friendship was harmless, she wouldn't need secrecy. Eventually, the emotional intimacy becomes undeniable.

> She tells him things she never tells her husband.
> She laughs harder with him than with her partner.
> She asks for his advice before she asks her partner's.
> She shares her pain with him, not with the man she married.
> He becomes the person she turns to when she feels unseen.
> The husband becomes the person who "just doesn't get it."

And then, it crosses the line.

> A hug lasts longer than it should.
> A hand rests on her waist.
> A compliment becomes flirtation.
> A moment of vulnerability becomes a kiss.

She will swear it "just happened." But emotional affairs never "just happen." They begin the moment she starts giving another man the intimacy, trust, and access that once belonged to her husband, and she refuses to see it as cheating because she is convinced the man is "safe."

Chapter 34

Sex During Business Trips: Conferences, Retreats, and Vacations With Friends

Sex on business trips is one of the most commonly underestimated forms of infidelity because it happens in a psychological vacuum: away from routine, away from accountability, away from the reality of home. The distance itself becomes permission. A woman leaves her domestic environment, puts on her professional or social "outside" self, and gains access to a version of her personality her partner rarely sees anymore. She dresses differently, behaves differently, and meets people who do not associate her with motherhood, responsibility, or routine. She becomes the person she used to be before commitment, or the person she always wished she were.

Business trips provide anonymity. The hotel room, the conference bar, the networking dinner—none of these spaces carry the weight of shared history. The people she meets do not know her husband, her children, or her past. They only see her in the moment: well-dressed, interesting, confident, desirable. A coworker or stranger can flirt with her without the emotional baggage of real life. The compliments land differently because they are not dulled by familiarity. They come from someone who finds her sexy not because he has to, but because he genuinely does.

The danger of trips and retreats is how effortlessly boundaries dissolve. Alcohol flows freely. Dinners lead to late-night conversations. Work colleagues share frustrations about careers, marriages, and identity. She begins to feel seen in a way she has not felt in years. She convinces herself she is simply networking, relaxing, decompressing. But then laughter becomes flirtation, flirtation becomes a touch on the lower back, a ride in an elevator, a moment of silence outside a hotel room door, and eventually a decision to step inside.

Women often rationalize this form of cheating as temporary or insignificant. They tell themselves, *It was just one night. We were both away. It won't happen again. It doesn't mean anything.* But sexual infidelity never exists in isolation. Even if it is only a single encounter, it represents a full emotional disengagement from the partner waiting at home. A spouse cannot accidentally end up naked in a hotel bed with a stranger or colleague. It requires a series of chosen steps, each one deliberate, each one a betrayal.

Trips with friends are no different. A woman surrounded by single friends, divorced friends, or friends who encourage her to "live a little," becomes susceptible to group permission. The rules loosen. The moral standard shifts. No one in that circle holds her accountable. They tell her she deserves fun, that her husband will never know, that she shouldn't waste her youth. It is not the alcohol that makes her cheat; it is the emotional permission granted by an environment where no one sees her marriage as sacred.

And when she returns home, she often compartmentalizes. She acts normal. She hugs her children, cooks dinner, asks about her husband's day. He will never smell cologne on her neck or find lipstick on her collar. The betrayal took place in another city, another hotel, another moment that will never exist again. But the damage is not physical; it is spiritual. She now knows she is capable of stepping outside the marriage without consequence. And once that door has been opened, it never fully closes again.

Sex during business trips is not an accident. It is the marriage left behind for a night, and often, in ways her husband will never discover, forever.

Chapter 35

Hookups With Exes: Comfortable, Familiar With Low Emotional Risk

Hooking up with an ex is one of the most deceptively dangerous forms of cheating because it masquerades as familiarity instead of betrayal. It feels safe to her because she has already shared a history with him. The boundaries were broken long ago; no barrier needs to be crossed anew. She does not have to build trust, flirt, or seduce someone from scratch. The groundwork is already there. All she has to do is step back into a dynamic she once knew well.

It usually begins with nostalgia disguised as casual contact. A message on a birthday, a "Hey stranger," a comment on an old photo, or a late-night conversation that reopens emotional doors. The ex becomes a reminder of who she was before marriage: younger, freer, desired. He remembers her body, her laugh, her vulnerabilities, her intimate details. He sees her not as a tired wife juggling responsibilities, but as the woman he once wanted. He does not need to peel through the layers of daily life to reach her; he already knows how she opens.

This familiarity becomes emotional anesthesia. There is no fear of judgment, no anxiety of rejection, no awkwardness of discovery. She convinces herself that it is harmless because "We already had history," or "It doesn't count if it's someone I was with before." The mind tries to rewrite betrayal into nostalgia, as if the past grants permission to trespass in the present. She tells herself the experience is easier because she doesn't have to pretend. He already knows her body. She already knows his intentions.

The danger is in how effortless it becomes. She does not have to flirt or pretend she is single. She does not have to build new chemistry, only revive old sparks. A visit to her hometown, a chance meeting, a lonely night when she feels misunderstood at home, a moment of weakness after a fight. The ex becomes a shortcut to validation. It feels like stepping into a warm bath she has been in before: comforting, familiar, guiltless in her mind. But the comfort does not erase the betrayal. It magnifies it.

With an ex, she does not cheat to explore. She cheats to escape. The encounter is controlled. She can walk into his arms without needing to impress him. She can let her guard down because he already has seen her at her most vulnerable. That makes the betrayal even more intimate. She is not experimenting with a stranger—she is returning to someone who once held her heart.

And when it is over, she tells herself it was meaningless because "We both moved on," or "It was just closure," or "It was a moment of weakness." But cheating with an ex is never meaningless. It is the clearest possible message to her husband: she chose to revisit a past lover instead of honoring the man she committed her life to.

Hookups with exes are not about discovery, passion, or temptation. They are about taking the easiest route to validation, using nostalgia as justification, and retreating into a version of herself that no longer exists. It is cheating wrapped in familiarity, and that makes it one of the most seductive and devastating forms of betrayal.

Chapter 36

Sex for Validation: Using Intimacy to Feel Wanted, Powerful, and Admired

Sex for validation is not about love; it is about identity. A woman who cheats this way is not searching for connection or partnership. She is searching for proof that she still matters, that she is still desirable, still attractive, still capable of turning heads and awakening hunger in someone other than her husband. Sex becomes a mirror she uses to check if she still exists.

This form of infidelity often begins quietly. She notices she is not being complimented as much at home. Her husband has become familiar, comfortable, distracted, tired. He stops noticing her hair, her clothes, the small efforts she once made to feel beautiful. She begins to wonder if she is invisible. Then a man outside the relationship makes her feel seen: a compliment, a lingering look, a flirtatious message. A moment where she is admired for no reason other than being herself.

The praise hits her like oxygen. Suddenly she feels alive again. She starts dressing differently, checking her reflection in the mirror with a different intention. She begins chasing that feeling, not the man, but the feeling of being wanted. And when she sleeps with him, it is not because she loves him. It is because she loves how she feels through him.

Sex becomes a performance. She chooses poses, lingerie, gestures not for romance or emotional connection, but to elicit a specific reaction: desire, awe, hunger. She wants to see a man lose control, shake, gasp, reach for her. Not because she cares about him, but because his reaction confirms her worth. She may sleep with someone younger to feel youthful, someone successful to feel valuable, someone bold to feel adventurous. Every encounter becomes a way of reclaiming a piece of herself she believes her husband has forgotten.

This type of cheating is addictive because validation is a drug. Once she learns she can generate adoration on command, the high becomes difficult to resist. She may chase multiple partners, not because she wants more sex, but because she wants more affirmation. Each encounter becomes a test:

> Can she still attract?
> Can she still seduce?
> Can she still command desire?

Each "yes" becomes a hit of dopamine that quiets the deep insecurity beneath it.

Afterward, she often returns home without guilt. She tells herself it meant nothing. There was no love, no emotional attachment, just physical affirmation. That makes it easier to justify. She convinces herself she was simply filling a void her husband created by neglecting her. She didn't betray him, she tells herself, she simply reminded herself that she matters.

The tragedy is that sex for validation never quenches insecurity. It feeds it. The more she uses other men to feel desired, the more dependent she becomes on the outside world to feel whole.

Her husband can never compete with that. He sees her every day. Familiarity dulls fantasy. No matter how deeply he loves her, he cannot recreate the intoxicating thrill of being the stranger who sees her for the first time.

Sex for validation is not a moment of weakness. It is a wound disguised as seduction. A woman isn't sleeping with another man because she is in love with him; she is sleeping with him.

Chapter 37

Digital Escorts/Cam Interactions: Paying or Receiving Sexual Attention Online

Digital infidelity is often dismissed because it has no physical contact, but it is one of the most potent forms of betrayal. When a woman exchanges sexual attention online—whether she is paying for it, performing for it, or receiving it—she is transferring her sexual energy to a space outside her relationship. The intimacy is real, even if the bodies never touch.

It often begins with curiosity or loneliness. She discovers a platform where she can be desired without consequence: private cam sites, OnlyFans subscriptions, online sex workers, virtual strip clubs, or even live chats with strangers. The anonymity of a screen gives her permission she would never grant in person. She does not need to flirt, seduce, or build a relationship; she can simply pay or participate and be sexual instantly. The experience becomes transactional, clean, and detached, at least in her mind.

What she does not realize is that digital intimacy is still intimacy. The man on the screen is seeing her body, hearing her voice, reacting to her gestures. If she is paying for sexual attention, she is rewarding a stranger for giving her something her husband may not provide: affirmation, hunger, excitement. And if she is the one receiving attention, performing on cam, exchanging pictures, doing custom requests; she has become the source of someone else's arousal. She becomes an object in someone's private fantasy, and she does so deliberately.

These interactions can feel safer than physical affairs because they avoid consequences that people fear: pregnancy, STDs, reputation. But the lack of physical risk makes them even more seductive. She can log in from her phone in the bathroom, from the living room while her husband sleeps, from a hotel room on a work trip. There is no travel, no effort, no planning. Just a few clicks and someone is begging to see her body.

Digital encounters also leave behind an illusion of control. She tells herself, *It's not cheating if I don't touch anyone*, or *It doesn't count because it's virtual*. But the truth is harsher: she is sharing her sexuality with someone who is not her partner. She may perform live, send pre-recorded videos, record audio clips, or pose in ways intended to arouse a stranger. The attention she receives becomes addictive. She begins to crave tips, praise, messages saying "You're perfect," or "You're the sexiest woman I've ever seen". Each notification reinforces the belief that she is desired by many and owned by none.

The emotional damage to her marriage is deep. Her husband is no longer the audience of her body; he becomes the person she hides it from. She spends more energy preparing outfits, makeup, and angles for strangers than she does for intimacy at home. She uses paid compliments to patch emotional wounds. And when he notices the secrecy, she calls him paranoid, controlling, or insecure, because exposing the truth would collapse the whole fantasy.

The most dangerous aspect of digital cheating is how casual it becomes. There is no awkward introduction or buildup of tension. She can cross sexual boundaries in minutes. She can be the aggressor, the seductress, the desired one, all without leaving her bed. And because there is no physical evidence, she can pretend nothing ever happened.

But infidelity is not defined by touch. It is defined by loyalty. If her body, her fantasies, her arousal, and her attention are being sold to, traded with, or given to other men—even through a screen—then she is already cheating. Digital escorts and cam interactions are not harmless entertainment; they are sexual betrayal wrapped in pixels and denial.

Chapter 38

Club Hookups: Kissing, Touching, Grinding, and Sexual Contact in Nightlife Settings

Club cheating is fueled by anonymity, alcohol, darkness, loud music, and the illusion that what happens in a crowded room full of strangers isn't real. A woman who has been feeling invisible at home steps into a nightclub and suddenly becomes the center of attention. Eyes follow her, hands reach for her, invitations surround her. She no longer feels like a wife with responsibilities; she feels like a woman desired in the moment, without consequence.

It begins with dancing. She isn't thinking about boundaries, loyalty, or marriage. She is thinking about the thrill of moving her body, the rhythm, the attention from men who stare openly. A stranger gets close. He places his hands on her hips. She leans back. The dancing becomes grinding—bodies pressed together, breathing against each other, pulses syncing with the music. No words are exchanged. They don't know each other's names. They don't need to. Their bodies speak for them.

Alcohol makes everything easier. It blurs guilt and sharpens impulse. She feels bold, untouchable, alluring. She thinks, *It's just dancing*, or *It doesn't matter if I'm not doing anything serious*. But intimate physical contact doesn't require sex to be sexual. Grinding is simulated intercourse with clothes on. Kissing in the corner of the bar is foreplay with strangers who will disappear by sunrise. Hands exploring her body on a dance floor are not "just harmless fun." They are the physical surrender of boundaries.

What makes club cheating especially dangerous is how fast it escalates. The environment is built for impulsive decisions. Dim lights hide the morality. Loud music blocks rational thought. Every woman is surrounded by men willing to take what her relationship no longer gives her: attention, compliments, hunger, mystery. A quick kiss between sets, a hand slipping up her thigh, a bathroom make-out session, a ride home offered by someone she just met—each step happens in seconds.

And she tells herself it isn't cheating because it is fleeting. She doesn't plan to meet him again. There are no conversations or emotional attachments. The encounter does not threaten to turn into a second relationship. She thinks, *It meant nothing*. But cheating doesn't need meaning to be betrayal. Sometimes the worst betrayals are the ones committed simply because she *could*.

What makes these encounters so devastating to her partner is the brutality of being replaced physically without even being remembered. The stranger at the club doesn't know her history, her sacrifices, her fears, or her goals. He doesn't love her, respect her, or want a future with her. He wants one thing: her body. And she gives it to him freely, without hesitation, without consideration of the man who loves her at home.

Nightlife cheating is also fueled by the culture of denial. She tells her friends, "Don't tell him." They tell her, "You're young. You deserve fun." The group becomes accomplices, not protectors. The morning after, she rewrites the night in her mind. She says she was drunk. She says she barely remembers. She says it wasn't that serious. She convinces herself her husband would overreact, not because it wasn't cheating, but because deep down, she knows it was.

Club hookups are not accidents. They are choices made under flashing lights and loud music, hidden behind alcohol and anonymity. They are the temporary surrender of loyalty in exchange for a moment of attention. They are sexual contact disguised as dancing, intimacy disguised as fun, betrayal disguised as freedom. And when the sun rises, the stranger forgets her name, while her husband wakes up believing he is still the only one who holds her.

Chapter 39

Using Dating Apps: "Just Talking," Curiosity, Flirting, Then Progressing to Sex

Dating apps are often the entry point to infidelity because they allow a woman to step outside her relationship without leaving her bed. She creates a profile, uploads flattering photos, selects a few prompts, and suddenly she is exposed to hundreds of men who want her. The experience is intoxicating. In minutes she receives validation that her partner no longer gives her: likes, messages, compliments, invitations, and attention. The modern digital marketplace turns her into a commodity with endless buyers.

It usually begins with curiosity. She tells herself she is "just browsing," that she wants to see if she could still attract someone, that she simply wants to understand what the dating world looks like. She has no intention of meeting anyone. She only wants to feel desired again. Swiping becomes a form of emotional gambling. Every match is a dopamine spike, a reminder that there are men out there who would eagerly choose her. The app becomes a secret mirror where she checks her sexual worth.

Then the messages start, and the denial begins to crumble. She engages in flirtation, playful banter, witty exchanges, inside jokes. The men she speaks to never hear the tone of her voice when she's tired, never see her messy hair in the morning, never deal with her stress or mood swings. They see only the best version of her: curated, polished, interesting, mysterious. She becomes addicted to that version of herself. She begins to compare these strangers' energy with her partner's routine. The husband becomes ordinary. The men online become exciting.

She insists it is harmless. She says, "We're just talking," or "It's not serious," or "I'm not meeting anyone." She conveniently ignores the fact that she is hiding the app, muting notifications, deleting chats, and lying about why her phone is always in her hand. She is no longer seeking to assess her attractiveness; she is seeking emotional stimulation, which she cannot find at home.

Inevitably, she escalates. Messages turn into private photos, late-night conversations, sexual jokes, fantasies. The man becomes real. His desire becomes tangible. She imagines what he would do to her, how he would touch her, whether he would appreciate her body in ways her husband no longer does. The boundary dissolves. The app is no longer a game; it is a gateway.

Eventually she meets someone. A coffee date, a casual drink, dinner "just to talk." She tells herself it is nothing serious. She convinces herself it is still harmless. But the truth is simple: no one meets a man from a dating app just to chat. She is already entertaining the possibility of sex. She had been mentally undressing him long before they ever stood in front of each other.

And then it happens: a night in his apartment, a hotel room, a parking lot, her best friend's house when she "stays over." The encounter feels thrilling, reckless, forbidden. She tells herself it was deserved, that her partner forced her into this by neglecting her, that she only did what any woman would do if she was unappreciated. But no justification changes the core reality: she has replaced her partner's intimacy with that of a stranger she met in an app designed to find new lovers.

The most painful part for her husband is that the betrayal began long before the sex. The moment she downloaded the app, created a profile, uploaded photos, and swiped—she chose to step out of the relationship. By the time she ended up in another man's bed, the cheating was simply the final act of a play she had been rehearsing privately for weeks or months.

Dating apps are not little games. They are pipelines from emotional curiosity to physical betrayal. And by the time she tells herself it "just happened," she has already crossed every boundary that once protected the sanctity of her marriage.

Epilogue

The Roads Back to Ourselves

nfidelity is often spoken about as a single moment: a kiss, a text, a hotel room, a lie. But in truth, it begins long before that.

It begins in the silent spaces, when admiration dries up, when appreciation becomes routine, when affection is replaced by obligation, when conversations stop being honest and start being safe.

Men and women may cheat differently, but they bleed the same. A man may stray when he no longer feels capable, respected, or admired. A woman may stray when she no longer feels cherished, understood, or seen. Both seek something they fear has disappeared, inside themselves or within their relationship.

Cheating is rarely about sex. It is about longing. It is about the hunger to feel important again, the craving to be noticed, the desperation to escape the version of ourselves we can't fix. It is about validation, attention, revenge, numbness, and the hope that someone else might finally make the pain quieter.

But understanding why we cheat is only half of the journey.

Because after the betrayal comes the mirror.

Some couples will never heal. The wound is too deep, the trust too shattered, the story too broken to continue. This is not failure—it is honesty.

Others choose to rebuild. Not because forgetting is possible, but because courage is. Repair does not mean returning to who you were; it means becoming who you never dared to be.

Forgiveness is not permission; it is release. It is choosing to stop punishing yourself for someone else's actions, or stop punishing another for the moment you lost your way.

Healing demands what infidelity avoids:

> **Awareness** — seeing the truth as it is, not as your ego paints it.
> **Intention** — committing to act with care instead of blame, humility instead of pride.
> **Repair** — restoring connection through action, rebuilding trust through consistency,
> and honoring your partner not through promises but through behavior.

At the heart of every betrayal is a person who didn't know how to ask for what they needed. Someone who feared rejection more than consequences. Someone who hoped a secret could fix what honesty might break. Some learn too late. Some learn just in time. Some never learn at all.

But if you are reading these words, you are not done. You are not hopeless. You are not beyond repair.

Let this book be a lantern, not a weapon. A guide, not a punishment. A reminder that love is fragile when neglected, not when imperfect. A reminder that loyalty is not automatic; it must be tended to like a living thing.

Infidelity is not the end of the story. It is a fork in the road. One path leads to bitterness, silence, resentment and blame. The other leads to awareness, intention, repair, and sometimes, rebirth.

You cannot rewrite the past. But you can choose how you live the rest of your life. If there is one truth to carry forward, let it be this:

> **Love does not collapse in a single night.**
> **It withers moment by moment—until someone stops tending it.**

Talk sooner. Listen deeper. Praise often. Honor your partner's dignity and guard their heart as if it were your own. And most importantly, repair what is broken *before* someone seeks comfort in the arms of a stranger. Because if you protect your relationship with Awareness, Intention, and Repair, you will never again mistake attention for love, nor mistake temptation for salvation.

About the Author

R.E. Geffner, MD, is a physician and relationship educator dedicated to helping people cultivate healthier, more resilient connections. He holds a bachelor's degree in biology, a master's in human anatomy from Rutgers University, and a medical degree from the New Jersey School of Medicine.

Dr. Geffner has seen how emotional stress, relational conflict, and unresolved personal struggles often manifest in physical symptoms. This intersection of medicine and human connection inspired his work as a relationship educator, where he blends clinical insight with a grounded, compassionate approach to navigating love, communication, and personal growth.

Drawing on decades of patient care and a lifelong commitment to understanding the human experience, Dr. Geffner offers a practical, empathetic perspective on the challenges that shape modern relationships. He divides his time between New Jersey and Florida, where he enjoys being on the water and remains active in the local maritime community.